NORTHWESTERN UNIVERSITY PRESS

MEDIEVAL FRENCH TEXTS

GENERAL EDITOR

NORMAN B. SPECTOR

NORTHWESTERN UNIVERSITY

THE ROMANCE OF

TRISTAN AND ISOLT

The Romance of Tristan and Isolt

TRANSLATED FROM THE OLD FRENCH

BY NORMAN B. SPECTOR

WITH A FOREWORD

BY EUGÈNE VINAVER

NORTHWESTERN UNIVERSITY PRESS

EVANSTON

1973

FOR BOBBY AND MIMI

CONTENTS

Foreword

THE LOVE STORY OF TRISTAN AND ISOLT WAS originally a "legend," not in the sense in which we now use the term, but in the literal sense of "something to be read"—a written composition which one of its earliest adaptors, Béroul, claims to have found in that form:

> ...comme l'estoire dit,
> La ou Berox le vit escrit.

It was, as far as we know, the work of a French poet of the second or third quarter of the twelfth century, no doubt incorporating a number of themes drawn from oral tradition but similar in form to the type of narrative which eventually came to be known as "romance." The work itself has survived only through its various adaptations, which include two twelfth-century French poems by otherwise unknown authors—Béroul and Thomas—and a French prose romance—*Tristan de Léonois*—written between 1225 and 1230 and preserved in a large number of manuscripts of the thirteenth, fourteenth, and fifteenth centuries. Until the rediscovery of the poems of Béroul and Thomas by nineteenth-century scholars, the story of Tristan was known to the modern world chiefly through this romance, which for six centuries enjoyed unrivaled popularity throughout Western Europe. Sir Walter Scott, who was the first to rediscover some fragments of the poem of Thomas, bestowed high praise upon the prose romance for its "art," and Alfred de Vigny wrote about it nostalgically: "Qui songe à ce roman du moyen âge? Personne; et il est délicieux."

Tristan de Léonois is a work of forbidding dimensions modeled upon the Arthurian prose romances which by that time had begun to eclipse the somewhat less sophisticated verse romances of the twelfth century. Only a small part of the work is a retelling of the original Tristan poem. The bulk of it is a typical Arthurian romance describing the protagonist's exploits in the service of knighthood and, ultimately, the Round Table. The manuscript tradition is vast and confused; so far it has eluded any attempt at strict classification, but one of the fifteenth-century copies of the romance, MS. 103 of the *fonds français* of the Bibliothèque Nationale, stands out for a variety of reasons: as a particularly fine example of fifteenth-century calligraphy, as the work of a well-known scribe, Michel Gonnot, to whom we owe some other equally precious volumes, and—last but not least—as the only manuscript of the prose romance of Tristan to have preserved the original (or "poetical") version of the story of the lovers' death. A very similar text was used by the French printers of the fifteenth and sixteenth centuries for the publication of the romance, so that it can safely be assumed that the *Tristan* which Sir Walter Scott and Alfred de Vigny knew and admired was not unlike MS. 103. But the dimensions of the work were such as to discourage any attempt to reproduce it in its complete form. Nowadays, only parts of it are available in print. In 1905 Joseph Bédier published in the Appendix to his edition of Thomas what he called the *parties anciennes* of MS. 103, and this carefully transcribed fifteenth-century text is still, apart from the early editions, the only reasonably complete record we have of the genuine medieval French Tristan romance. Few, if any, nonspecialists have had occasion to see it, and since no other French text can claim the same degree of completeness and authenticity—the surviving fragments of the poems represent in each case less than a third of the whole work—one cannot help wondering what people have in mind when they speak in a general way of the "legend of Tristan and Isolt." Probably a combination of well-known modern works such as Wagner's opera, Swinburne's *Tristram de Lyonesse,* and Bédier's own free adaptation of the story, *Le Roman de Tristan et Iseut.* By translating into English the *parties anciennes* of MS. 103, Professor Spector has at long last remedied this anomaly. The lay reader can now have access to a complete and faithful account of the most widely known of love stories.

A number of misconceptions may now be corrected. It is likely that certain things in the following pages will strike the reader as being curiously out of keeping with what he has imagined the Tristan story to be. He will find that it is neither a portrayal of what has come to be known as "courtly love" nor a story of romantic love written to glorify an all-powerful passion which deliberately flouts social convention. It is a tale of tragic love, enacted as it were above the level of the characters' consciousness: a tale of a disaster caused by the clash of irreconcilable forces, human and supernatural. The magic of the love potion is no less powerful than the sense of feudal and moral allegiance binding the lovers to the world from which they find themselves exiled for a time—a world from which there is no final escape but death. When the green and leafy bramble that springs from Tristan's tomb finds Isolt's grave on the other side of the chapel, no human hand can prevent it from uniting the lovers in its embrace; but while their lives last what power on earth can ever set them free? Tristan is a king's son and Isolt a king's daughter. A romantic hero and heroine would have escaped either to his kingdom or to hers, proclaiming in this way the sovereign right of their love to rule their destiny. Not so the two lovers of Cornwall. Found guilty of treason, they live like outcasts in the forest of Morois:

Tristan rode along all lost in thought. And when he had reflected he said to Queen Isolt, "Lady, what shall we do? If I take you to the kingdom of Logres, I shall be called a traitor and you a disloyal queen. And if I take you to Lyonesse, everyone will blame me and say that I am keeping the wife of my uncle" (pp. 49–50).

This juxtaposition of two equally uncompromising forces dominates the action from the moment the lovers drink the potion. It does so here as it did in the original verse romance and in Béroul's adaptation. But there is this important difference: that while Béroul, following the original poet, conveys significance through objects, real or supernatural—the potion, the rings, the weapons, the physical signs of hardship endured by the lovers, the forest hut replacing Isolt's royal chamber—the prose writer expresses the same tensions and contrasts through the words spoken by the characters. The story, he feels, has to be made explicit by the utterances of the characters themselves; it has to be consistent with their thoughts and feelings. Such a notion may seem obvious to us, but it was a novelty in twelfth-century France, when it first established itself as the distinguishing feature of the more rational type of narrative. In the Prose Romance of Tristan we can see the meeting point of this newly developed narrative technique with the original conception of a love story forced as a result into an unfamiliar mold; for we are here on the threshold of a new literary tradition even while we still experience the fascination of the old. Dialogue is consistent with action, which it explains and sometimes prompts, as the case may be; and motivation through character brings about some important changes in the whole nature of the work. In the *parties anciennes* King Mark is still a loving husband and an affectionate uncle, averse

xvi

to the horrible punishment which the law of the land forces
him to inflict upon the lovers; but as soon as we leave the
original story he becomes a villain, a traitor, and a murderer.
In all the surviving versions of the Prose Romance other
than MS. 103 and the early printed editions, it is he who
causes Tristan's death by stabbing him in the back with a
poisoned spear sent to him by Morgan le Fay. For those who
favor this kind of rational order there can be no better
denouement: the hero *must* die at the jealous villain's hand.
But no such order exists in the original poetical version or in
the one preserved in MS. 103, and any sensitive reader will
surely agree that its absence is one of the great assets of our
text; the story of the lovers' death as told here has miracu-
lously escaped the impact of the "explanatory" trend. And
whenever the rhetoricians try to persuade us that a denouement cannot be valid unless it arises naturally from the plot
and the characters of the story — *du sein même de la fable*, as the
old manuals used to say — the example of the Prose *Tristan*
can serve to make us aware of their limitations. *Or dit li
contes* — this traditional opening of a paragraph in almost
any medieval prose romance establishes an essential hierar-
chy: at the beginning is the story — *li contes*. It is told by an
author whose only task is to transmit the story to his readers
or listeners; and last of all there are the dramatis personae
fashioned by both the story and the author. *Their* task is to
serve the story, not to direct it or even interpret it. In the
earliest Tristan romance, so much of which survives in the
pages of MS. 103, all that the poet wanted us to know about
King Mark and the two lovers was what they did, not who
they were or what they might have done in other circum-
stances; and any attempt to account for the action of the tale
as though it were dependent upon them is doomed to fail-

ure. It is the action alone that makes them live and confers upon them a true sense of poetic reality.

This is the reason why they all seem to speak with one voice—a voice which is not their own, but the author's, marked by subtle rhythms and cadences, like much of the old French secular prose of the time. Only a translator such as Professor Spector, with his impeccable sense of the resources of both languages, could have reproduced that voice with so little sacrifice of its original character. Nothing comparable exists among the recent attempts to render old into modern French prose. The work was considered in the Middle Ages—witness Brunetto Latini's famous eulogy—a masterpiece of literary prose, and it is not too much to say that this translation brings us closer than any previous endeavor of its kind has done to the literary experience that until now has seemed to be the exclusive privilege of medieval readers.

EUGÈNE VINAVER

Translator's Preface

THE ROMANCE OF TRISTAN PRESENTED HERE is a translation essentially of those portions of MS. BN 103, *fonds français,* which reflect the so-called *version commune* of the Tristan story, and which relate the following episodes: the birth of Tristan, the adventure of the Morholt, the healing of Tristan by Isolt, the fight against the serpent and the winning of Isolt for Mark, the love potion and secret love of Tristan and Isolt, Isolt's near-murder of Brangien, the abduction of Isolt by Palamedes, the denunciation of the lovers by Andret, the trap of the scythes, the escape from the stake and the leap from the chapel, the flight to the forest of Morois, the recapture of Isolt by Mark and the wounding of Tristan, Tristan's flight to Brittany and his healing by Isolt of the White Hands, Tristan's marriage to Isolt of the White Hands, Tristan's involvement in the love affair of Ruvalen and Gargeolain, Tristan the Fool, Tristan's fatal wounding at the hands of Bedalis, the death of Tristan and Isolt.

To these materials has been added one adventure (from MS. BN 757, folios 38–40) not contained in MS. 103, the episode of Mark concealed in the laurel tree.

Despite their episodic structure, evident as well from the transitional synoptic material given in brackets, these extracts from MSS. 103 and 757 constitute a coherent narrative of the Tristan romance. It is my purpose, in translating them, to make available in English for the first time a narrative which reflects the primitive form of the story.

The translation is as literally close to the French texts as I could make it, with the single exception of a consistent transposition of the so-called historical present. The story thus runs continuously in the past, as distinguished from the transitional synoptic materials presented in brackets. The decision to follow the Old French closely is based on two aims: to render the text as accurately as possible, and to make access to the original texts easier for the nonspecialist reader by providing him with a tool to facilitate his acquisition of a reading knowledge of Old French. It is my intention to publish in the near future a new edition of the Old French texts which constitute this version of the romance. In the meantime, the interested reader will find the Old French texts in Appendix 1, "Les Parties anciennes du roman en prose française," of Bédier's edition of *Le Roman de Tristan par Thomas, poème du XIIe siècle*, Société des Anciens Textes Français (Paris, 1905), pp. 321–95.[1]

The present volume is not the place for extensive analysis of the Tristan and Isolt legend as presented in MS. 103, but the illuminating foreword which Professor Eugène Vinaver has kindly provided furnishes a background and perspective that all readers and students of the romance will find indispensable. I should like to express my gratitude to Professor Vinaver for embellishing the enterprise with this lovely appreciation. Any shortcomings in the translation are, of course, the responsibility of the translator alone.

I should also like to thank Mrs. Annie Pardo for her rapid, accurate, and efficient typing of the manuscript.

---

1. The relationship of the episodes of the *version commune* to the vast prose Tristan romance is studied in E. Löseth's *Le Roman de Tristan en prose, le roman de Palamide et la compilation de Rustician de Pise: Analyse critique d'après les manuscrits de Paris*, Bibliothèque de l'Ecole des Hautes Etudes, 82 (Paris, 1890). Pertinent references to this work are given following the synoptic materials presented in the text in brackets.

The Romance of
Tristan and Isolt

*[A powerful king named Mark reigns in Cornwall.
Méliadus, king of Lyonesse, a country located in
Great Britain, comes and offers him his services.*[1] *He
marries King Mark's sister, Blanchefleur, and takes
her back to his country. Some time later, Blanchefleur
gives birth to a son and dies the same day.]* (Bédier, II,
194–95; Loseth, p. 16.)[2]

1. The name Méliadus appears in MS. 103. Elsewhere he is called Pivalen or
Rivalen. See J. Bédier, *Le Roman de Tristan par Thomas, poème du XIIe siècle,*
Société des Anciens Textes Français (Paris, 1905), p.194; hereafter cited as
"Bédier."

2. E. Löseth, *Le Roman de Tristan en prose, le roman de Palamide et la compilation
de Rustician de Pise : Analyse critique d'après les manuscrits de Paris,* Bibliothèque de
l'Ecole des Hautes Etudes, 82 (Paris, 1890); hereafter cited as "Löseth."

THAT DAY AND NIGHT THE QUEEN LABORED. AT dawn she delivered herself of a fine son to the will of Our Lord. And, when she was delivered, she said to the maiden, "Show me my child and I will kiss him, for I am dying."

And she gave him to her. And, when she held him, she saw that he was the fairest child in the world and she said,

"Son, much have I desired to have you. Now I see in you the fairest child that woman ever bore, to my knowledge. But your beauty will do me little good, for I am dying of the labor which I have had of you. Sad I came here, sad I lay in bed to bring you forth, in sadness have I had you. And the first rejoicing that I have had of you has been in sadness, and for you I shall die sad. And, since in sadness you have come to earth, you shall have the name Tristan. May God grant that you live your life in greater joy and good fortune than your birth has brought you."

And, when she had said this, she kissed him, and, as soon as she had kissed him, the soul left her body, and she died as I have told you. Thus was born Tristan, the fair, the good knight who afterward suffered so many sorrows for Isolt.

The king took the child and gave him in charge to Gouvernal, who took care of him in such loyalty that none could reproach him and procured a proper nurse for him . . . .

[*Tristan is raised and educated by Gouvernal. After many adventures, the two come to Cornwall.*] (*Bédier, II, 195–96.*)

But now the story stops telling of Tristan and King Méliadus, his father, and speaks of King Mark . . . .

THE COMBAT WITH THE MORHOLT

Now there was imposed on those of Cornwall each year a tribute of a hundred maidens and a hundred youths of the age of fifteen and a hundred prize horses. And this tribute was established in the time of King Thonosor of Ireland, and it lasted two hundred years. And it was paid each year without fail until the time of King Mark. But in that time the tribute failed, for the fair Tristan, the good loving knight, fought on account of it with the Morholt, brother of the queen of Ireland, who had come to Cornwall to demand the tribute and who was killed on the isle of Saint Samson, as our story will tell later.

Tristan [had come] before King Mark, his uncle, and offered his service. And the king asked him who he was.

"Sire," he said, "I am a youth from a far country who would serve you, if it please you."

"It pleases me well," said the king, "for you seem to me indeed of noble birth."

Tristan stayed with his uncle as a man from a foreign land, and he accomplished so much in so little time, that no youth in the court was esteemed worth a cent compared to Tristan. If Tristan went to the woods to perform his service, he was esteemed above all his companions. The king would go nowhere without him. Tristan undertook nothing that he did not succeed in well and wisely to his great contentment and for his fair service, in which all the youths of the court did not envy him, for all were put back on account of him.

Tristan served until he reached the age of fifteen. Then he was so accomplished and so strong that none had his prowess or swiftness. Gouvernal rejoiced greatly that he had grown and developed so, for henceforth he could be a knight. And, if he were, he could amount to great things.

And so it happened, as I tell you, and all without fail, that at the beginning of May the Morholt of Ireland and many men with him came to Cornwall to seek the tribute that those of Cornwall owed the king of Ireland....[3] And in that time the reign of King Arthur had begun, but it was only a little while since he had been crowned. When those of Cornwall heard that those of Ireland had

3. MS. 103 alludes here to the presence of the Morholt's companion, Gahariet, who does not figure elsewhere in the Tristan-Isolt story as here presented.

come to seek the tribute, then began the mourning and the wailing up and down the land. The mourning of the ladies and knights began, and they spoke thus of their children,

"Children, in misfortune were you born and raised, when those of Ireland must take you in servitude to their country! Earth, why have you not opened and swallowed up our children? It would have been better for our honor than that those of Ireland should take you into servitude! Criminal and cruel sea and treacherous wind, why have you not blown and blasted so as to drown them all in the sea?"

Thus they carried on in their sorrow, so that one could not have heard God's thunder. Tristan asked a young knight why they were lamenting so and who was this Morholt of whom they spoke. And the knight told him that the Morholt was brother to the queen of Ireland, one of the best knights in the world, who had come to seek the tribute. And he had been sent there so that if anyone gainsaid him he would fight with him on this account and defeat him in hand-to-hand combat. And there was none who dared go against him, for he was much too good a knight.

"And if someone," said Tristan, "overcame him at arms, what would be the outcome?"

"Faith," said the knight, "Cornwall would be freed of the tribute."

"In God's name," said Tristan, "then can it easily be freed, when through the person of a single knight they can be delivered."

"They cannot," said the knight, "for there is no man in this country who would dare fight him."

"Faith," said Tristan, "then are those in this country the most cowardly knights in the world!"

And then Tristan went to Gouvernal and said,

"Master, those of Cornwall are wretches, for there is none so bold who dares fight the Morholt to free them of the tribute. Certainly, if I were a knight, I would fight with him to prevent the servitude. And, if it pleased God that I win, all my lineage would be honored, and I would be more esteemed for it all my life. But

7

what is your opinion of this? Here I can put to the test whether I will ever be of valor. And certainly, if I am not, it is better that the Morholt kill me and that I die at the hand of so valiant a man of such renown than that I live with the wretches of Cornwall, and I would have greater honor."

Gouvernal, who loved Tristan as much as anything on earth, said,

"Tristan, fair sweet son, you have spoken well. But the Morholt is a knight such as none in the world, and you are so young and have learned nothing of the art of chivalry."

"Master," he said, "if I do not undertake this enterprise, have no faith that I will ever be a man of worth. And it comforts me greatly that you have told me and made me understand that my father was one of the best knights in the world. And I must resemble him by nature. Indeed, if it please God, I will not fail."

When Gouvernal heard this, all his senses were amazed, and he said,

"Fair son, then do as you will."

"Master," he said, "much thanks."

Then came Tristan before the king, his uncle, who was in a rage, for it had angered him greatly to find out that there was no knight in his castle[4] who dared fight against the Morholt in order to protect the tribute of Cornwall. But there was none so bold who dared stand forth. And here came Tristan, who kneeled before his uncle and said,

"Sire, I have long served you as best I could. I pray, as a reward for my service, that you make me a knight today or tomorrow. So long have I delayed that those of your court are blaming me for it."

The king answered,

"Fair friend, willingly will I make you one, since you request it of me, but in greater joy would I do so for you were it not for this mishap of those of Ireland, who bring us ill news."

4. The text reads: "car il s'estoit courouchié savoir moult s'il eust chevalier en son hostel...."

8

"Sire," said Tristan, "now do not be dismayed, for God will deliver us from this peril and others."

The king raised him by the hand and led him to Dynas, his seneschal, and told him to seek and equip him with all that he would need, for he would make him a knight the next day. That night Tristan kept vigil in a church of Our Lady. The next day King Mark made him a knight as honorably as he could. And know that those who saw him said that never did they see so fair a knight in Cornwall.

As they were rejoicing in the celebration for Tristan, there came four wise and well-spoken knights on behalf of the Morholt, and they said to the king without greeting him,

"King Mark, we have come here on behalf of the Morholt, the best knight in the world. And we ask you for the tribute that you owe each year to the king of Ireland. Arrange to have it for him within six days. Otherwise we challenge you on his behalf. And if you anger him, there will remain to you not a square foot of land, and all Cornwall will be destroyed on account of this."

The king was so distraught when he heard this news that he did not know what to say. And Tristan sprang forward and said,

"Lord messengers, tell the Morholt that never will there be any tribute, for if our ancestors were so mad and foolish, we are wiser and we will no longer pay for their foolishness. And if the Morholt says that tribute is owed him, I am ready to do combat with him for it hand to hand, so that those of Cornwall may be free and owe him nothing. If I kill him, we are quit. And if he kills me, he will have the tribute by right."

And the messengers said to the king,

"Does this knight speak for you?"

"Faith," said the king, "I had not ordered him to say this, but since such is his will, such is my faith in God and in him that I grant him the combat."

[*Tristan then reveals that he is the son of King Méliadus of Lyonesse and King Mark's nephew. The*

9

messengers report to the Morholt, who sends them
back to inquire about the site of the combat. They
choose the isle of Saint Samson, where the two com-
batants are to go alone, each in his boat. Mark
expresses his sorrow, informing Tristan that had he
known his identity he would not have permitted him
to fight. The combat is set for the next day and the
night is spent in prayers. Tristan keeps vigil in a
church of Our Lady. He goes to bed near dawn. When
he awakes, the king arms him and he embarks. The
Morholt offers him his friendship, which he rejects.]
(Bédier, II, 326; Loseth, p. 20.)

... Then they let their horses charge toward each other, and they
struck each other so sorely with their lances that they bent sharply.
And know that they would have killed each other if the lances had
not shattered. And they hit each other breast to breast so cruelly
that they flew to the ground, so stunned that they did not know
whether it was day or night. And nevertheless they rose, sorely
wounded. Tristan was wounded by the tip of the Morholt's spear,
which was poisoned, and the Morholt was likewise wounded by
the tip of Tristan's spear. But it was not poisoned. Then they drew
their swords and they struck each other as hard as they could, so
that shortly they were spent and weary from the great blows that
they had given each other. And no armor that they had could
prevent them from inflicting great and marvelous wounds on
each other, so that they lost blood copiously. The Morholt, who
thought that he was one of the best knights in the world, feared
Tristan's sword so greatly that he was amazed. And know that
Tristan feared the Morholt greatly also. And those who watched
them from afar said that never had they seen two knights of such
strength. And much did they fear each other. And nevertheless,
since they had agreed that one must conquer the other, there was
no mercy. And they came together, bare sword in hand, and they
struck each other more harshly and more cruelly than ever they
had done. And such blows did they strike at each other that the

healthiest man in the world could hardly have come away from them alive. In such great rage Tristan struck a blow with his sword on the Morholt's helmet that the blade cut through to his head. And from the shock of the blow a great piece of the sword blade remained in the Morholt's head, so that the sword was separated from it.

When the Morholt felt that he was mortally wounded, he threw down his shield and sword and turned in flight to his boat and entered it and departed as rapidly as he could. And he came to his men, and they received him on their ships, sorrowful and in rage at this adventure. He said to them,

"Let us embark at once and set sail for Ireland. I am wounded to death, and I greatly fear that I shall die before we arrive."

Then they obeyed his command and made ready and set sail. When those of Cornwall saw them go, they cried out, saying,

"Go and don't come back! May a bad storm drown you all!"

King Mark saw his nephew, Tristan, all alone on the isle, who had won his battle, and he shouted to his men,

"Bring me Tristan, my nephew! God has indeed favored us greatly by his mercy. Through Tristan's prowess is Cornwall today delivered from its servitude."

Then they ran to the boats and came to the isle, and they found Tristan so weak that he could scarcely stand from the blood he had lost. And they put him on a boat and they took him to the king. And when the king saw him, he kissed him more than a hundred times and asked him how he was.

"Sire," he said, "I am wounded, but if it please God I shall recover."

The king took him to the church to give thanks to Our Lord for the honor he had done him. Then they went back to the palace to great rejoicing and festivity. Tristan went to lie on a bed, for he was in such pain from the poison of the venom that he could neither laugh nor rejoice nor eat nor drink.

THE VOYAGE TO IRELAND

The physicians came to see him, and they placed herbs on his wounds in various ways, so that in a short time he was cured of all his wounds, except the one where the venom was. But of this one he could not be cured, for the herbs were contrary to it, and they were unaware of the poison of the venom. Tristan was in such pain and anguish that he slept neither day nor night and scarcely ate or drank, and he wasted greatly away. His wound stank so that none could remain close to him except Gouvernal, who served him steadfastly. He wept for Tristan and lamented him so, that it was a pity to see him. For any who had seen Tristan before would not have recognized him, so badly had he changed. All the nobles were sorrowful and said,

"Ah, Tristan! How dearly have you bought Cornwall's freedom! Ah, sweet Tristan, what a loss we have in you! You will die in sorrow of what is now our ease!"

One day Tristan was on his bed, so thin and pale that none who saw him could but feel pity. A lady stepped forward, who wept bitterly and said,

"Tristan, I marvel, fair friend, that you do not take counsel of yourself. You can neither die nor recover. Certainly, were I in your place, I would go to another land, since I could not recover in this one, to find out whether God or another would devise a way to cure me."

"Lady," said Tristan, "and how could I do this? I could not ride, nor could I suffer to be borne on a litter."

"Faith," said the lady, "then I cannot advise you. May God counsel you."

Then she departed straightway. And Tristan had himself carried to a window looking out on the sea and began to look at the sea and thought for a long time.

And when he had finished his thinking, he called Gouvernal and said,

"Master, go to my uncle and tell him to come and speak to me."

And he went and said,

"Sire, come and speak to Tristan."

And the king went and said,

"Fair nephew, what is your pleasure?"

"Sire," said Tristan, "I ask a boon of you which will cost you little enough."

"Certainly," said the king, "if it were to cost me a great deal, I would give it to you, for there is nothing in this living world, no matter how great, that I could have in any way that I would not do for you."

"Sire," said Tristan, "I have suffered great pain and anguish since I fought the Morholt for Cornwall's freedom. I can neither die nor live in this land. And since it is so, I wish to go to another land, if it please God, to find out whether God would rather send me a cure in another land than this one."

"Nephew," said the king, "and how would you go to another land? You can neither ride nor walk, nor could you suffer to be borne on a litter."

"Uncle, I will tell you how I will do it. You will have a small boat built for me with a little sail that I can raise and lower by myself when I wish, and there will be a canopy of silk above for the heat and the rain. And you will have food put aboard on which I can sustain myself for a long time. And you will put my harp and my rota on board, and all my instruments, with which I may divert myself at times. And when it is ready, you will have my bed put in it, and then you will have me carried there, and then you will launch me to sea. And when I am at sea all alone, without company, and none will know me there, then, if it please God that I drown, death will please me, for too long have I languished. And if I recover, I shall come back to Cornwall. Thus do I wish it to be done. And, in order to have it done as soon as possible, I beg of you with folded hands that you hasten to have it done without delay, for never again shall I have joy until it is done and I am at sea."

Then, when he had spoken thus, the king began to weep and said,

"What, fair nephew, then do you wish to leave me?"

"Certainly, uncle," said Tristan, "there can be no other way."

"And what will become of Gouvernal? If he is with you, he will be a great comfort to you."

"Certainly," said Tristan, "from this point on, I will have no company other than God. But if I die, I desire that he have my land, for he is indeed of such high lineage as to be a king, after having received the order of chivalry."

The king saw that it could not be otherwise, and he had the little boat prepared as Tristan had said. When the boat was furnished and equipped, they bore Tristan on it and placed him inside. But never was seen such great sorrow as there was for the departure of Tristan. When Tristan saw this great grief, it pained him much to remain, and he had himself launched out to sea, with his sail set. And in a short time he was so far away that neither did he see his uncle and friends nor did they see him.

Thus did Tristan travel by sea, and it was two weeks or more before he arrived one day at Ireland before the castle of Hessedot. The king of Ireland and the queen, sister of the Morholt, were there, and Isolt, their daughter, and they were dwelling there. Isolt was the most beautiful woman in the world and the wisest in surgery known to exist in that time, and she knew all herbs and their powers. And there was no wound so dangerous that she could not cure. And she was no more than fourteen years old.

When Tristan came to port and saw the land that he did not know, his heart rejoiced in him on account of the new land. And because God had cast him up out of the peril of the sea, he took his harp and tuned it, and he began to play it so sweetly that none who heard it would not willingly have listened. The king was at his window, and he heard the sound and saw the boat so well furnished, so that he thought it was magic. And he pointed it out to the queen.

"Sire," she said, "God keep you, let us go and find out what this can be."

Then the king and queen went down all alone without com-

pany from the court, and they came to the shore and listened to
Tristan play his harp until he had played all his music and set his
harp down before him. Then he asked the king what land this was
where he had arrived.

"Faith," said the king, "this is Ireland."

And he was more ill at ease than before, for he knew well that if
he were recognized, he would have to die on account of the
Morholt whom he had killed. The king asked him who he was.

"Sire," he said, "I am from Lyonesse, near the city of Albisme,
an unfortunate and ill man who has sought his fate in this sea. I
have come here to find out whether I might find a cure for my
illness. For so much anguish and pain have I suffered as none could
suffer more, and I would rather die than languish long in this
pain."

"Are you a knight?" asked the king.

"Sire, yes," said Tristan.

Then the king said,

"Then do not be dismayed, for you have arrived at such a port
where you will find a cure. For I have a daughter most wise, and if
anyone is ever to cure you, she will do so in a short time. And I
shall ask her to undertake to do so for the sake of God and for pity's
sake."

"Sire, may God keep you for it!" said Tristan. Then the king and
queen went off to their palace. The king called those within and
ordered them to go to the port and fetch an unfortunate knight
and bring him back and make a fine bed for him and place him on
it. And they did as he commanded them. When Tristan was in
bed, the king told Isolt, his daughter, to take care of the knight.
And she did so very gently and watched over him and looked to
his wounds and put herbs on them. And she told him not to be
dismayed and that she would make him well soon with the help of
God.

In this chamber Tristan lay ill for ten days. The damsel cared for
him each day, but each day he did but get worse, for the herbs
were contrary to him. When Isolt saw this, she was astonished and

15

cursed her wisdom and her knowledge and said that she knew nothing of what she thought she knew better than anyone in the world. And then she reflected and said that his wound was poisoned with venom and that [she knew] what would not fail to cure it, and that with this she would cure it swiftly. And if it were not poisoned, she said that she would never lay a hand on it, and it would be a lost cause. Then she had him brought out into the sunlight so as to see the wound more clearly. And when she had seen the wound, she said that it was poisoned with venom, and she said,

"Ah, sire, the point [of the spear] that gave you this wound was poisoned. This is what has prevented those who should have cured you, for they were not aware of the poison. But I have seen it now, and, if it please God, I shall bring you back to health. Of this be certain."

And Tristan was overjoyed at this news. The damsel obtained for him what was needed and what she thought best to remove the venom. She took such pains and labored so that she rid him of it completely, and Tristan began to recover and to eat and drink and regain his beauty and strength. So well did the damsel work that before two months had passed Tristan was as hale and hearty as he had ever been. Then he thought that he would go back to Cornwall, for he knew well that if he were recognized, they would make him die in shame and pain on account of the Morholt, whom he had killed.

[*However, Tristan does not return at once to Cornwall, but goes to the tournament of the Castle of the Clearings. Palamedes is introduced here, who falls in love with Isolt. Victor in the tournament, Tristan returns to the castle of King Angyn of Ireland.*]
(*Bédier, II, 332; Loseth, pp. 21–24.*)

16

THE COMBAT WITH THE SERPENT

In that country there was and dwelled a serpent, which ravaged and destroyed the whole country and came to the castle about twice a week and devoured and ate all those it could seize, so that none dared leave the castle on account of the serpent. The king had proclaimed that to whoever could kill the serpent he would give whatever he asked, indeed the half of his kingdom and Isolt, his daughter, if he would have her. And it so happened that the serpent came to the castle the very day that the king had proclaimed this proclamation. And each one who went out of the castle, of those who lived in it, fled back into it, crying and screaming. And Tristan asked what this was. And he was told what I have told you and the proclamation that the king had had proclaimed.

When Tristan heard this, he put on his armor so quietly that none knew of it. Then he went out of the castle by a postern gate and went on until he saw the serpent. And, as soon as the serpent saw him, it rushed upon him and Tristan toward it. And so began the hard, cruel battle of Tristan and the serpent. The serpent sank its claws into his shield and tore the thongs and everything it touched. And it shot fire and flame at his face, so that it burned all of his shield and almost knocked him to the ground. And Tristan regathered his strength and raised his sword and struck the serpent. But he found its hide so hard that he could not make the sword penetrate. Then he struck again with a thrusting blow. And the serpent came at him with its maw gaping to eat him. And Tristan saw it and shoved the sword down its throat into its belly and cut it open from heart to belly in two pieces. And then the serpent lay dead. And Tristan cut out its tongue and shoved it into his breeches. Then he departed, but he had hardly gone a step when he fell to the ground as though dead, on account of the venom of the serpent's tongue that he had in his breeches.

King Angyn had a seneschal, called Aguynguerren the Red. He, on his way to the castle, found the slain serpent and cut off its head and said that he would present it to the king, and then ask him for his daughter and half of his kingdom, and then make the king believe that he had killed the serpent. The seneschal came to the king, showing the head of the serpent, and greeted him and said to the king,

"I have killed the serpent for you that was destroying all of this country. Here is its head. Now I ask you for Isolt, your daughter, and half of your kingdom, as you have promised."

The king marveled much at this and said,

"Seneschal, I will speak to Isolt, my daughter, and find out what she thinks of this."

And then the king went into the queen's chamber and found the queen and Isolt, his daughter, together. And he told them that the seneschal had killed the serpent,

"...and has brought me its head. Now I must keep the promise that I had proclaimed."

And when the queen and Isolt heard this they were sorely angered. And Isolt said that he would never have her and that she would rather be dead than that this treacherous redheaded felon should ever have her.

"But, sire, you will go to him and tell him that you will take counsel with your barons on this matter and that you will be able to tell him the truth of it in a week."

Then the king went back to the seneschal and told him these words that I have said to you, and the seneschal agreed.

And the queen said to Isolt, her daughter,

"Daughter, let us, you and I, quietly go and see the serpent that is dead, for I do not believe the seneschal to have been so bold as to attack the serpent."

"Lady," said Isolt, "willingly."

Then they went off all alone except for two squires, Perinis and Mathanael. And they walked until they saw the slain serpent and looked at it a long time. Then they turned back and looked at the side of the road and saw Tristan there, lying as though dead. And he was as swollen as a barrel. And they went to the spot, but they did not recognize him because of the swelling. And Isolt said,

"This man is dead or poisoned by the serpent, and I believe that he has killed the serpent and the serpent him."

Then, for pity's sake, and with the help of the two squires, they managed to carry him off to their chambers, and there he was stripped of his clothes and the serpent's tongue was found in his breeches. Isolt felt his body and found that he was still alive, and she made him drink some theriac and took such care of him that all of his swelling went down and he was cured and restored to his beauty. And they saw that it was Tristan, their knight, and they were full of joy.

At the end of a week the seneschal came back to the king and asked him for his boon. And the king took counsel with his barons, and the barons said that he should grant it, since he had promised. When Isolt heard this she began to lament sorely and said that she would let herself be torn limb from limb before he had her or she gave herself to him. And while she was lamenting thus sorely, Tristan came and asked her what was the matter and why she was sorrowing so. And she told him that the seneschal would have her for his wife "...and half my father's kingdom because he said that he killed the serpent."

When Tristan heard this, he said,

"Now do not be dismayed, in that I will indeed deliver you from this, for he is lying. But now tell me if you know where the tongue is that I had put inside my breeches when I was brought here."

"Sire," said the queen, "here it is."

And Tristan took the tongue and went to the palace and said, with all listening,

"Where is the seneschal who will have Isolt and says that he killed the serpent? Let him come forward, for I say that he is lying and am ready to prove it against him in hand-to-hand combat or otherwise if need be."

And the seneschal sprang forward and said that he had done so. Then Tristan said to the king,

19

"Sire, look inside the serpent's head to see whether there is a tongue, for I tell you that he who killed it cut out its tongue."

And then the head was examined and no tongue was found. And Tristan showed the tongue, and it was joined to the place from which it had been removed, and it fitted perfectly. Then the seneschal was shouted down and seized and slain. And Tristan was honored and served when it was learned that he had killed the serpent.

It happened one day that Tristan was bathing. The queen and Isolt and Brangien and many others were in his presence and served him very courteously. A youth, kin to the queen, came there and looked on a bed and saw Tristan's sword that was so richly adorned, the one with which he had killed the Morholt. And he drew it from the scabbard and saw that it was breeched, and he was amazed. And the piece had remained in the head of the Morholt, and the queen kept it wrapped in a cloth of silk in a case. And as the youth was looking at the sword, the queen came there and asked whose sword it was. And he answered that it belonged to Tristan, who was bathing there.

"Indeed," she said, "then take it into this chamber."

And he took it in. And the queen opened her case and unwrapped the piece of sword that had been found in the head of the Morholt, and she joined it to it, and it was exactly like the one that had [been] shattered at the blow when Tristan killed the Morholt.

"Ah, God!" said the queen. "This is Tristan who killed my brother. Long has he hidden from us. With this sword he killed him and with this sword he shall die."

Then she came to Tristan, who knew nothing of this, and cried,

"Ah, Tristan, nephew of King Mark, it was no use to hide! You are dead! You killed my brother by your hand with this sword, and with this sword you shall die!"

Then she raised the sword and made as though to strike. And Tristan did not budge or give any semblance of fear. And a squire leaped forward and seized the queen and said,

20

"Ah, Lady, for the mercy of God, do not kill the best knight in the world in this way. It is not proper for you to do this, who are a lady. Let the king decide on this, who will indeed avenge you."

And the queen would not hold back, and nevertheless he restrained her. And the shouting and the disturbance were so loud that the king and his barons came at the noise. And the queen said to him,

"Ah, sire, here is the traitorous murderer, Tristan, who has hidden so long from us, who killed the Morholt, my brother. Either you will kill him or I shall. Here is the very sword with which he killed him, and with this sword I want him to die."

The king was wise and thoughtful, and he said,

"Lady, be silent. Leave this vengeance to me, and I shall do it in such a way as none can blame me."

"Sire," she said, "much thanks. You have saved me!"

"Give me that sword," said the king.

And she gave it to him and then left the place. And the king came to Tristan and said to him,

"Are you Tristan, who killed the Morholt?"

"Sire," said Tristan, "there is no use hiding it. I am indeed he. If I killed him, none must blame me, for I had to do it. For he would have killed me, had he been able."

"You are dead," said the king.

"You may do this," said Tristan, "if you will. In your hand is my death or my life."

"Then get dressed," said the king, "and come hence to the palace."

And Tristan dressed and went thence to the palace. And when he was before the barons, he was somewhat ashamed, and he began to blush, and he was even more handsome on account of it. And those who looked at him said that too great harm would be done if so fair and good a knight as he were to receive death for a matter that could not be repaired. And the queen cried out to the king,

"Sire, avenge me on Tristan, the traitor, who killed my brother!"

21

And the king said,

"Tristan, you greatly shamed and debased me when you killed the Morholt, and [yet] great harm would be done if I killed you, for I would not do so for this. I will let you live for two reasons. One is on account of the good chivalry that is in you. The other is that you have been brought back from the point of death in my house. And, since I have healed you, if I were then to kill you, it would be an act of great treachery. Now, leave my house and my land at once and never be found in them again, for if I were to find you there once more, I would put you to death."

"Sire," said Tristan, "much thanks for the great kindness you do me."

Then the king had him given arms and a horse, and he mounted and departed. And Brangien secretly brought him her two brothers, who would willingly serve him. The queen was very sorrowful and angry at Tristan's going off so free and clear, for she greatly desired his death.

Tristan went off to the port and put out to sea and sailed until he reached Cornwall at Tintagel, where King Mark was. When the king and the barons saw Tristan, there was as much rejoicing and festivity as if Our Lord had descended to earth there. The king asked Tristan how he had accomplished this. And he told him how he had been cured and how Isolt the blond had healed him and how he had been in peril of death. But he did not tell them how he had been the victor at the assembly and had defeated Palamedes, nor how he had killed the serpent. And then he told him how Isolt the blond, the fairest damsel in the world and the wisest in surgery, had cured him. Those of the place rejoiced much at this news, and there were great festivity and rejoicing. The king made him master and lord of his house and of whatever he had, and because of this he was held in greater fear and apprehension than he had been before.

[Tristan has a love affair with the wife of Count Segurades, a lady of whom Mark is also enamored.

22

*Mark, jealous, begins to hate his nephew. One day he
makes him swear to tell all the chivalrous deeds he has
done, and he thus learns of Tristan's exploits in
Ireland.] (Bédier, II, 337; Loseth, pp. 25–27.)*

THE LOVE POTION AND THE MARRIAGE

The king was ill at ease on account of Tristan, for now he feared
him more than before. And he thought that he would willingly
put Tristan to death, if he could, in such a way that it would not be
apparent to him. And [he thought that] if he dismissed him from
his court, it would go ill for him. And if he kept him with him, he
was so loved by all that if great strife should arise between them he
would have the worst of it in the judgment of the case. And he
thought about this, for he saw no way out anywhere. And an idea
came to him that rejoiced him greatly, for by means of it, as he
thought, he could rid himself of Tristan. And he would die, which
mattered not to him, for he would rather have him dead than
alive.

Shortly thereafter, it happened that the king was sitting in the
midst of his barons, and Tristan was there in his presence. The
barons said to the king that it was a great marvel to them that he
did not take a wife. And Tristan said that it would please him
greatly if he had a wife. And the king said,

"Tristan, I will have one when it pleases you, for it is up to you
to obtain such a fair one as you know I would have her."

"Sire," said Tristan, "since it is up to me, you shall have her, for
I would rather die than that you should not."

"How shall I believe you?" asked the king.

And Tristan stretched his hand out toward a chapel and swore
that with God's help and his blessing he would do everything in
his power. And the king thanked him greatly.

"Now I will tell you the one I wish," said the king. "You know
indeed, and many times have you told me so, that if I were to take
a wife, I should take such a one in whose beauty I could take

23

delight and solace. And in the matter of beauty you have praised only one woman to me, and this one you have affirmed to be the most beautiful in the world. This one do I want, and this one shall I have if ever I am to take a wife, and she is Isolt the blond, daughter of King Angyn of Ireland. This is the one you must bring me as you have promised to do. Now take from my household such company as you wish and set forth and pursue this undertaking until I have her."

When Tristan heard this news, he thought that his uncle was sending him to Ireland more for his death than to obtain Isolt, but he dared not refuse. And the king, who wished him ill rather than well, said to him in honeyed tones,

"Fair nephew, will you not bring her to me here?"

"Sire," said Tristan, "I shall do everything in my power to do so, were I to die for it."

"Fair nephew, much thanks," said the king. "Now you must get on with it, for I shall never have joy until you have come back and have brought Isolt the blond with you."

Tristan would have withdrawn willingly from this affair if he could have done so. But there was nothing to be done, for he had taken an oath before many a noble, and therefore he was silent. And he knew full well that he was being sent there to die, for it was the one place in all the world where he was most hated on account of the Morholt whom he had killed.

"Then let it come out as it may," he said [to himself], "all according to chance."

Then he took forty knights, young men of the highest lineage who were in King Mark's household. These were very sorrowful and angry and would rather have lost all their lands than that the king should send them to Ireland, for they knew full well that if they were recognized they should all be killed. Then they made ready and embarked, and Tristan and Gouvernal also. And Gouvernal wept hard for Tristan and said,

"Now you can see how much your uncle loves you. This thing is planned for your death and not to obtain the damsel."

"Fair master," said Tristan, "now do not be dismayed. If my uncle hates me, I shall do so much by my good deeds, if it please God, that his heart will not be so cruel toward me as not to wish me well. And let him not be dismayed, for I will so accomplish it, if it please God, whatever be the pain, that I shall have the damsel."

"May God grant it!" said Gouvernal.

And so Tristan put to sea with his companions, who were greatly dejected because they were going to their death, as it seemed to them. But Tristan comforted them and told them not to be dismayed in any way. And they had such trust in him that they were all reassured. For it seemed to them that no harm could come to them in any place where he was....

> [*A storm casts Tristan and his companions on the coast of Britain. At Arthur's court he again meets Angyn, the king of Ireland, and performs valuable service for him by replacing him in single combat against a fierce knight. In exchange, Tristan obtains from him the promise of a boon. And, in fact, Angyn takes him back to Ireland and asks the queen and Isolt to pardon him finally for the death of the Morholt.*]
> (*Bédier, II, 339; Loseth, pp. 27–28.*)

"And" [said the king of Ireland], "were it not for the great valor in which Tristan is so perfect, as you know, he would have been killed and I would have been destroyed. And, since he has done so much for us and is with us, let us think to serve and honor him and return to him the kindness that he has done us."

"Sire," said the queen and all the others in one voice, "we have all been asked to do this, and we desire henceforth that the kingdom of Ireland and that of Cornwall be friendly and have good will toward each other."

Then there was rejoicing and great festivities were arranged for Tristan and his companions. And he remained with Isolt, who cared for his wounds until he was agile and well. And when he was healed and recovered and he saw the beauty of Isolt, which was so great that it was a byword near and far, his heart was transformed and given over to shifting thoughts. And he said that he would ask for her for himself and not for another. For if he had her, he would have the fairest lady in the world, and she would have the fairest knight and one of the best in the world. Then he said that he would have done great treachery to his uncle, for he had promised her to him before many a noble. And this would always be to his shame, for he loved his honor more and would rather let her go than have her to his shame.

One day when the king had come to his palace, Tristan came before him, and along with him his companions nobly appareled, and he said,

"King, I desire you to give me my boon."

"Certainly," said the king, "this is right. Ask and you shall have it."

"Sire," said Tristan, "much thanks. Now then give me Isolt, your daughter. And know that I do not ask her for myself, but for King Mark, my uncle, who desires to have her for his wife and will make her queen of the kingdom of Cornwall."

And the king answered him and said,

"Tristan, you have done so much for me that you have earned the right to have Isolt. And I give her to you, either for yourself or for your uncle. You may do in this as you will, for this pleases me greatly."

Then he had Isolt come, and he led her to him by the hand, and he said,

"You may take her from here when you will, for I feel you to be such a loyal knight that you will never do anything that will turn to villainy."

Now Tristan received the damsel for King Mark, his uncle. Then such great festivities began there as if God had descended on earth. For those of Ireland rejoiced, and it seemed to them that through this marriage peace would be made between them and those of Cornwall. And those of Cornwall were greatly delighted, for they had accomplished their task without great pain and were honored and served in the one place in the world where it had been the custom to hate them most....

[*There follows the account of a foreboding dream of the king of Ireland.*] (*Bédier, II, 340.*)

When Tristan had properly and completely equipped himself for his voyage, the king gave Isolt to him and several damsels with her who would keep her company. And know that Isolt departed well furnished with robes and jewels, so that it would be apparent to all that she came of high station. The king and queen wept at the departure. The queen called Brangien and Gouvernal and said to them,

"Here is a silver vessel full of a marvelous potion that I have prepared with my own hands. And when King Mark will lie with Isolt the first night, give it to King Mark to drink, and afterward to Isolt, and then throw away what is left. And see to it that none other drink of it, for great ill could come of this. And this potion is called the love potion, for as soon as King Mark will have drunk of it and my daughter afterward, they will love each other so strongly and so marvelously that none will be able to bring discord between them. And I have prepared it for the two of them. Therefore see to it that none other drink of it." And they said that they would see to it.

Thereupon they departed. And Tristan and his company put to sea and went off in great joy. For three days they had good winds. On the fourth day Tristan was playing chess with Isolt, and it was so hot that Tristan became very thirsty, and he asked for wine. Gouvernal and Brangien went to get it for him, and they found the love potion among the other silver vessels, of which there were many. And so they were undone, for they took no note of it.

Brangien took the cup of gold and Gouvernal poured into it the drink, which was clear as wine. And wine it was indeed, but other things were mixed with it. Tristan drank deep from the cup and then ordered that it be given to Isolt, and it was given to her. And

Isolt drank. Ah, God, what a drink! And then did they enter the path that they would never again leave in their life, for they had drunk their ruin and their death. The drink seemed good and most sweet to them, but never was sweetness bought so dear as this would be. Their hearts changed and were transformed. As soon as they had drunk, they looked at each other all in amazement. Now they thought of other things than they had done before. Tristan's thoughts were of Isolt and Isolt's of Tristan. Forgotten was King Mark. Tristan thought only of having Isolt's love and Isolt only of having Tristan's. In this their hearts were united, so that they would love each other all their lives. And, if Tristan loved her, this was according to her will, for in none fairer or better could she use or place her love. And, if Tristan loved Isolt, this was according to his will, for in none fairer could he have placed his heart. He was most fair, and so was she. He was of gentle birth and she of high lineage. Indeed did they match each other in beauty and in lineage. Now let King Mark seek another queen, for Tristan would have this one, and Isolt would have him. So long did they gaze at each other that each knew the will of the other. Tristan knew well that Isolt loved him with all her heart, and Isolt knew well that Tristan hated her not. Great was his delight in what had happened, and great was her joy. He said that he was the most fortunate knight that ever was, since he was loved by the fairest damsel who would ever be henceforth in all the world.

When they had drunk the love potion, as I have told you, Gouvernal, recognizing the vessel, was struck dumb. And so sorrowful was he that he wished he were dead. For now he knew full well that Tristan loved Isolt and Isolt Tristan, and he knew full well that he and Brangien would be blamed for it. Then he called Brangien and told her that they had been undone by their blunder.

"How?" asked Brangien.

"Faith," said Gouvernal, "we have given Tristan and Isolt a drink from the love potion, and now must they perforce love each other."

Then he showed her the vessel that contained the drink. And

28

when Brangien saw that this was the truth, she wept and said,

"Ill have we performed our task. Of this can come only evil."

"Already do we suffer it," said Gouvernal, "and indeed we shall
see to what end this will come."

Gouvernal and Brangien were in sorrow, but those who had
drunk the love potion were in joy. Tristan looked at Isolt and
became so enamored and inflamed [with love] that he desired no
other thing but Isolt, and Isolt desired nothing but Tristan. Tristan
uncovered his heart to her and said to her that he loved her more
than any living creature. And Isolt said that so did she him. What
shall I tell you? Tristan saw that Isolt was willing to do all that was
in his will. And they were all alone, so that they had no hindrance
nor fear of each other. And he did with her according to his will
and took from her the name of maiden. In this fashion, as I tell it to
you, did Tristan fall into love of Isolt, so that in no day of his life
did he ever leave it, nor love another, nor know any other woman.[5]
And through this potion that he drank did he have henceforth
such suffering and pain that never before nor afterward was there
a knight who suffered such pain for love as did Tristan.

Gouvernal asked Brangien how it seemed to her of Tristan and
Isolt. And she said that it seemed to her that they had been
together, "...and Tristan has surely deflowered her. I saw them
lying together. King Mark will put her to shame when he does not
find her as she should be. He will have her destroyed and us with
her who were to have guarded her."

"Now do not be dismayed," said Gouvernal. "Since it is so, I
shall get you out of it. Now let me see to it, for you may be sure
that I shall work it so that we will never be blamed for it."

"May God will it," said Brangien.

Of this counsel Tristan and Isolt knew nothing. Instead, their
life was good and joyous, and they loved each other so that they
did not see how they could be apart a single day. And thus they

5. Tristan does not consummate his marriage with Isolt of Brittany until just
before he departs for his last meeting with Isolt the blond (see below, p. 67)

went on straight to Cornwall. But they would have come there sooner had a storm not carried them off.

> [*The storm carries them to an island, to the Castle of Tears, where they have several adventures. Finally they are able to set sail again.*] (Bédier, II, 343; Loseth, pp. 30–35.)

Now the story tells that when Tristan put to sea and departed from the Castle of Tears he sailed until he came to Tintagel, where King Mark was. And Mark was told that Tristan, his nephew, had arrived and that he had brought Isolt. When the king heard this, he was angry, for he had wanted never to see him again. And nevertheless he feigned joy and ordered that they go to meet him. The barons went up to meet Tristan and they welcomed him in great joy. King Mark kissed Tristan and all his other companions. Tristan came to the palace and took Isolt by the hand and said,

"King Mark, here is Isolt, whom you asked of me in this palace. I give her to you."

"Tristan," he said, "much thanks. So much have you accomplished that all must praise you for it."

Because of the great beauty that he saw in Isolt, King Mark said that he would marry her. Then he had all his barons summoned to come to the festivities at Tintagel, for he would wed Isolt and crown her with the kingdom of Cornwall. The barons, ladies, and damsels came from all around on the day that the king married Isolt. Great were the joy and festivities of those of Cornwall.

Tristan called Gouvernal and Brangien and said to them,

"What shall we do? You know well how it is with me and Isolt. And if the king does not find her a maiden, he will straightway have her killed. And I shall kill the king immediately and myself afterward, if you do not find a plan."

And Brangien said that she would give to it whatever thoughts were in her power.

"Faith," said Gouvernal, "now I shall tell you what you will do.

When the king is in his bed, you will extinguish the candles and you will go and lie with the king, and Isolt will be close to the bed. And when the king has had his will of you, you will get out of the bed and Isolt will get into it."

And Brangien said that she would do all according to their will for them and to save her lady.

Great were the festivities, as I have told you. Night came, and the king went to his bed. When he was in his bed, Tristan extinguished the candles, and Brangien lay down beside the king. And Isolt was by the bed.

"How, now," said the king, "why have you extinguished the candles?"

"Sire," said Tristan, "this is the custom in Ireland, and so I was ordered to do by Isolt's mother, for when a man of noble birth lies with a maiden, the candles are extinguished."

Then Tristan and Gouvernal left the chamber. And the king took Brangien and found her to be a maiden. And then he withdrew from atop her. And Brangien left the bed and Isolt entered it. In the morning the king arose and summoned Tristan, and he went to him. And the king said to him,

"Certainly, Tristan, you have guarded Isolt well for me. And therefore I make you henceforth my chamberlain and desire that you be master of my household. And after myself I award you the lordship of Cornwall."

And Tristan thanked him for it. The king had not noticed the exchange that had been made on him nor had he perceived anything.

[For a time, the lovers keep their love secret and none suspect them. But one day the thought comes to Isolt that Brangien, possessor of her secret, might denounce her to the king, and she decides to have her killed.]
(Bédier, II, 240.)

Great was [Mark's] love for Isolt, but she loved him not at all.

31

Rather did she love Tristan, with all her might. And if she behaved agreeably toward King Mark, it was only so that he should be aware of nothing between her and Tristan, and so that their love might not be noticed. Isolt feared nothing other than that Brangien might expose her, and so she thought that if she were dead she would fear no one. And so she called two servants whom she had brought from Ireland and she said to them,

"Take Brangien into that forest for me and kill her, for she has done a thing that displeases me. She has lain with the king."

And they said that they would willingly do her command. Then the queen called Brangien and said to her,

"Go into that forest with these two youths and gather herbs for me."

"Lady," said Brangien, "willingly."

Then off to the forest went Brangien and the two servants. And when they had come to the deepest part of it, one of them said to Brangien,

"Brangien, what have you done to Isolt, who wishes to have you killed?"

Then they drew their swords on Brangien. And when she saw this, she was afraid, and she said,

"Lords, may God help me, never have I done anything wrong to her that I know of, other than that when my lady, Isolt, left Ireland, she had a lily flower that she was to present to King Mark, and one of her damsels had another. My lady lost hers, for which it would have gone ill for her, when the damsel presented to him through me her own, which she had well guarded, and thus my lady was saved. And I believe that on account of this kindness she wishes to have me killed, for I know no other cause. And for the sake of God, if it please you, do not kill me, and I promise you faithfully that I will go away to such a place that neither you nor my lady shall ever hear of."

And they had pity on her, and they tied her to a tree and left her there with the wild beasts, and they bloodied their swords on an animal that they caught. Then they returned to Isolt. When she

32

saw them, she asked them whether Brangien was killed.

"Yes, lady," said the servants.

"And what did she say at her death?" asked the queen.

"Lady," they said, "nothing, other than these words."

Then they told her what I have related to you before. And when the queen heard this, she was so distraught at Brangien's death that she did not know what to say. She would have given whatever she had in the world for her not to be dead. And she said to the servants,

"Certainly her death grieves me greatly. Go back and bring me her body." And they went back, but they did not find her.

And now the story stops telling of her servants and returns to what happened to Brangien. Now the tale tells that when the servants had left Brangien and had tied her to the tree, she began to cry out so loudly that she was heard from afar. Now an armed knight came along....

[*The knight is Palamedes, who frees Brangien and takes her to a convent. He then informs Isolt, who now regrets what she has done, that Brangien is not dead, and the queen promises to give him anything he asks if he will return her safe and sound. Palamedes brings Brangien back and claims his boon of Isolt, who refers him to King Mark.*] *(Bédier, II, 345; Loseth, pp. 35–37.)*

"Now you may ask freely for anything you please, for I promise you as king that you shall have it."

"Sire," said [Palamedes], "thanks to you. And I ask you for my lady Isolt, the thing that I love most in the world."

When the king heard this speech, he was so astounded that he did not know what to say or do, and he said,

"Ah, sir knight, for the sake of God, ask something else of me, for I should be ashamed if you took the queen away."

"That is to no avail," said Palamedes, "for I would not take half

33

the kingdom of Logres for her, because I would rather be poor with her than rich with another."

The king saw that he could not unsay it, since he had granted it to him, and he said,

"I grant her to you. But, after I have delivered her to you, if she is taken from you, ask nothing of me in this matter."

"Sire," said Palamedes, "if a knight can take her from me in single combat, freely may he bring her back."

"Then take her," said the king, "by such a covenant that it may ill befall you."

Then he had the queen's palfrey made ready and had her mount it, and then he gave her to Palamedes and said,

"Lady, go wherever it is the will of this knight. You, yourself, have sought this."

Then the queen mounted, all in tears. And the king forbade that any knight be so bold as to go after her. And Palamedes and the queen departed. And the king was so angry that he did not know what to say.

Tristan was not there. Instead, he had gone hunting. Gouvernal, who had seen all this, said,

"Ah, Tristan! So much have you lost today, for there is none here so bold as to dare save my lady, the queen. Ill would they save another when they thus allow their lady to be taken off by a strange knight. Ah, Tristan, if you were here, three knights would never take her away...."

[*That evening, Tristan, back from the hunt, learns of Isolt's abduction, goes after her, wins her back, and after a short idyll with her, returns her to the court: "And Tristan returned to King Mark his wife and told him to watch over her better the next time, for with great difficulty had he rescued her. And the king thanked him for it."*] (*Bédier, II, 346; Loseth, pp. 36–37.*)

One day Tristan and Isolt were alone in King Mark's chamber.

34

Andret,[6] who hated Tristan very much and who had become aware of their love, came to King Mark and told him that he was the basest and most wretched man in the world, since he suffered on his land the one who was putting him to shame with his wife.

"Who is he?" asked the king.

"Sire," said Andret, "it is Tristan. I have been aware of it for some time, but I have not told you because I thought that he would correct his ways."

"And how shall I know this to be true?" asked the king.

"Go straight to your chamber," said Andret, "and you will find them there alone."

> [*The king, hoping to surprise the lovers, rushes to his chamber, sword in hand. But Gouvernal warns Tristan, who avoids Mark's sword stroke, responds in kind, and fells the king with the flat of his sword. Tristan flees into the forest. The king, following Andret's advice, recalls Tristan in an apparent reconciliation in order to trap him later.*] (*Bédier, II, 347; Loseth, pp. 37–38.*)

Tristan spoke to the queen whenever he could, but this was not very often, for the queen was watched too closely. She was guarded with all his might by Andret, who swore to King Mark that if Tristan came to the queen and were by any chance found with her, he would kill him if ever he could, and he would never hesitate to do so. And the king said to him that never would he be so grateful to him as for putting Tristan to death, if it should happen to come about. What should I tell you? [The king] saw and realized from the looks that Tristan gave the queen and she him whenever they were at table that they still loved each other as madly as ever. And truly they loved each other then so sorely that never had they burned so nor been so desirous of one another as

6. Here MS. 103 reads Sandret. Other spellings of the name of this character, who is presented as the son of Mark's sister, are Antret and Audret. See Bédier, p. 245.

35

they were then. The king was so angered by this that he was dying of rage and spite. He hated Tristan with such a mortal hatred that never was he content when he saw him. And if he could have brought about his death in any way, he would have sought to do so only too willingly. But he did not see how he could do it easily, for Tristan was too good and noble a knight.

Tristan gave himself over to joy and delight and was happier than he had ever been, for never were they able to guard the queen so well that he did not speak to her every time. The king saw this clearly, and it sorrowed him so that he wished he were dead. And if anyone were to ask me where they spoke together, for the tower was so well guarded that never could he get in without too great harm, I would say that they came to each other in a garden that was at the foot of the tower. The garden was fair and big, and in it was a great quantity of trees of various kinds. But among the other trees was a laurel so fair and so tall, that in all of Cornwall there was not a tree so fair. Under this tree there was a lovely spot, and many times did the two lovers come there when it was night and all were at rest. And they talked there together and did freely as they wished.

Andret, who was greatly galled by this affair and who would willingly have brought about Tristan's death if ever he could, found out about it before anyone else. He learned that they were meeting in the garden beneath the tree. He came to the king and told him. The king sorrowed greatly at this news. He did not know what to do, for he greatly feared to attack Tristan on account of the good chivalry that he knew was in him. Nor would he lay hands on the queen in any way, for he loved her no less than he did himself. And Andret said to him anyway,

"Sire, what will you do in this matter?"

"Now, leave it to me," said the king, "for I believe that I will indeed take care of it myself, and in such a way that my honor will be completely spared...."

THE LAUREL TREE

[*One evening, Mark climbs the laurel tree, armed with bow and arrows, resolved to kill Tristan. The latter arrives first at the rendezvous with Isolt and, thanks to the bright moonlight, sees and recognizes Mark in the tree. Isolt also recognizes the king in time.*] (*Bédier, II, 348.*)

"My lord Tristan," she said, "what is your pleasure? You sent word to me, it seems, to come here and speak to you. I have come, as is plain. What do you wish? Certainly I have taken a great risk in coming here. For you may be sure in truth that if King Mark knew it, he would have me put to shame, for he would sooner think that I had come for ill than for good. For long enough the evil tongues of Cornwall have given him to understand that I am madly in love with you and you with me. I do love you sincerely and shall love you all my life, as a good lady should love a noble knight, according to God and according to the honor of her husband. God knows well and you, yourself, know how I have loved you according to God, and that you have never sinned with me nor I with you."

"Lady," said he, "you speak the truth completely. Constantly have you brought me honor, for which thanks to you, and have done me much more honor than I have deserved. And for the honor which you have so unceasingly brought to me you have often been ill rewarded, for the wretches and traitors have given my uncle to understand such things as I had not done nor would do for half the kingdom of Logres. God knows well, who knows and understands all, that never have I had thoughts of [loving] you in lustful love, nor shall I have such thoughts, if it please God. But most unwillingly would King Mark, my uncle, believe me in this."

"Certainly," she said, "if you loved me as madly as he thinks, then you would be the most disloyal knight in the world."

37

"Lady," he said, "you speak the truth. May God on high keep me from such an act and such a thought!"

"Now tell me," she said, "why you sent word to me last night that I should come speak to you."

"Lady," he said, "I shall tell you. The truth was that when we left the kingdom of Logres, it was agreed between me and my uncle that whatever there might have been between the two of us, he would never have an evil heart nor ill will toward me, and he forgave me for all of his bad feelings. Now he has given me to understand again that he seeks my death, and on this account I sent word to you in all sincerity in accord with God and reason. And therefore I pray you that if you know that the king holds me in mortal hatred, as I am told, you let me know. For in that case I would keep away from him and would leave this country, for I would rather be away from Cornwall all my life than kill the king through some misadventure."

The queen was most delighted and overjoyed when she heard these words. For she knew well from what my lord Tristan was saying to her that he had noticed that the king was up in the tree. And she spoke after a while, and she said,

"My lord Tristan, to what you ask of me I certainly do not know how to respond. You tell me that you have been given to understand that King Mark seeks your death with all his might. Certainly of all this I know nothing. If he wishes you ill and hates you, it is no great wonder, for the traitors in Cornwall, who are envious of the one whom all hold to be the best knight in the world, hate you so mortally that they never say anything but ill of you. And the king holds you in mortal hatred on this account, as I believe. And this is a great sin and sorrow, and if he knew the truth of your nature and your love, as God knows and as we ourselves know, he would love you above all men on earth and me above all ladies in the world. But this is not the way things are. He hates you, and me as well. Not that you deserve it, but so it pleases my lord."

"Lady," said my lord Tristan, "this hatred pains me sorely, especially because I have not deserved it."

38

"Certainly," said the queen, "it weighs heavily on me as well. But, since it cannot be otherwise, I must suffer it and look to the will of the king and the destiny that God has judged for me."

"Lady," said my lord Tristan, "since you tell me that the king hates me mortally, I shall go away from Cornwall to the kingdom of Logres."

"You shall not," she said. "Stay on. Perhaps the king will be reconciled better than he has been until now and will spare you his ill will. It would be great shame for you if you left this land so hastily, and the traitors in Cornwall would then say that you had left out of fear and lack of courage. In the meantime, God will send you some better counsel than you have had."

"Lady," he said, "then I will stay on."

"Indeed," she said, "that is my advice."

Thereupon the conversation ended. Tristan took leave of the queen and returned to his lodging, happy and joyous that they had had their conversation in this way in the presence of King Mark. For King Mark would henceforth not think so ill of the matter as he had before. The queen would be less closely guarded, Tristan would have more of King Mark's love, and the traitors would be less heeded in the matter. In this way he would not be prevented from taking Queen Isolt away from Cornwall the next day or afterward, if the occasion arose, for the queen would be only too willing. And this was a thing that comforted him greatly.

When the queen had left Tristan, she went to her chamber and found Brangien, who was awaiting her. All the other damsels were asleep, who knew nothing of this matter.

"Brangien, Brangien!" said the queen. "You do not know how it came out for us. You may be sure that the greatest adventure that ever yet happened to a lady came to me this night, and from King Mark himself."

"Lady, for God's sake!" said Brangien. "Tell me!"

"I will tell you," said the queen, "that King Mark came to spy on us in this way. And it happened, thank God, that we noticed him, and we changed our behavior and our words on the spot."

And she told her how and in what manner "...we got out of it, for I know in all certainty that King Mark henceforth has no bad intentions toward the two of us. On the contrary, he is resentful toward all those who ever spoke to him of this: Now you will see Andret in very bad standing at court. King Mark will never again think well of him, but will hate him with all his heart. Tristan the fair will now come to the forefront and Andret will be cast back. Blessed be the hour when this night came, for this night shall be the cause of our remaining in joy for a long time!"

Great was the joy and great the celebration between the queen and Brangien. After a while, the king came. And when the queen heard him coming, she got into bed and pretended to be sound asleep. The next morning the king rose quite early and went to hear mass in his chapel. Then he came back to his palace, and as soon as he saw Andret, he took him into a chamber. And Andret said to him immediately,

"Sire, how does it seem to you about Tristan and the queen?"

"This is the way it seems to me," said the king. "I have seen so much that I now know in truth that you are the most disloyal knight and the worst traitor that ever was in Cornwall. You made me believe and kept telling me on every occasion that Tristan, my nephew, was shaming me with my wife. This is the greatest lie in the world. If Isolt behaves warmly toward Tristan and honors him, she does not do so out of any lustful love that she feels for him, but first of all for the sake of God and out of courtesy and on account of the good chivalry that is in my nephew. So clearly have I seen this between the two of them that I shall forevermore love Isolt and Tristan, my nephew, and I shall hate you with all my heart because you falsely made me believe their disloyalty. Tristan is the most loyal knight I know and the best in the world, as everyone knows. You are the most disloyal knight in all of Cornwall. Therefore I tell you, on whatever I hold from God and all of chivalry, that were you not related to me by flesh and blood I would put you to such shame that there could never be any redemption from it. Now leave my household, for it pleases me not to ask any service of you henceforth nor that you should ever come here again."

When Andret heard this news, there was no question of his sorrow and anger. The king told him to depart and he did so, for he dared remain no longer, because he was in sore fear of the king. The king sent for Tristan, and he came to him happy and joyous, for he was sure that he would hear news pleasing to him. The king spoke, in the presence of his entire household, and spoke aloud so that all might hear.

"Tristan, fair nephew, what shall I say to you? I have hated you until now above all knights in the world, for I believed in truth that you were a traitor and that you sought my shame with the one I love most after myself. I have tried your loyalty in such a way that I know in all truth that you love me in true love, and that you have guarded my honor with all your might, and that all those are liars who kept making me believe that you were disloyal. I wish them ill and shall do so all my life, for through their counsel and opinion I have inflicted much dishonor on you, for which I now sorely repent. For to such a good knight as you are no man should do dishonor for anything that happens in this world. And, since I have done so out of bad judgment and through my sin, I implore your forgiveness for it and pray that you, yourself, will say what amends I must make in whatever fashion you wish."

To these words my lord Tristan replied and said,

"Sire, since you recognize that the shame you have sometime done to me you did not do so much out of your own design as through being incited to do so by the traitors in Cornwall, who kept making you believe lies about me, and you say that you repent of it, I forgive you for it willingly, in the presence of all the noble men who are here, in such fashion that you will promise me henceforth as a king that you will not again seek my shame nor suffer that I come to harm through any intention of yours." And the king promised him this in good faith.

Thus was the king reconciled with Tristan and Tristan with the king. All the noble men of Cornwall rejoiced and celebrated greatly at this. The traitors were sorrowful and angry, but the noble men were happy and joyful. Tristan had all that he wished, for he could speak with his lady whenever it pleased him. He found none who could forbid or gainsay him anything. He was entirely the lord and master of King Mark and Queen Isolt, and so feared was he in Cornwall that all his commands were carried out. The traitors were dying of envy and sorrow. They were so sorrowful and angry that they did not know what to say. Andret now stood so ill with the king that he dared not come to court, and he found none who would call for him. For all knew full well that the king hated him with all his heart. Tristan had his joy to the fullest and Queen Isolt as well. They could henceforth do nothing which displeased the king. The king had such trust in Tristan that he would have no one guard Isolt except him. Now did the two lovers have joy and solace and all good fortune. Never had they been as contented as they now were. For when they recalled the pain and torment that each had suffered alone, and they now saw themselves together and could do all they wished, they said that they would indeed have been born to good fortune if they could forevermore live in such joy and festivities. They would indeed have given up all claim to God's paradise to live such a life evermore.

THE SCYTHES

[*Andret is restored sufficiently to Mark's good graces to be readmitted to court. He resumes his plotting against the lovers and prepares the trap of the scythes.*]
(*Bédier, II, 158–59; Loseth, pp. 39–40.*)

Andret, who wished Tristan and the queen ill, and who would willingly have taken them together, had scythes prepared and put them at night before the queen's bed, so that if Tristan came there, he would mark himself in such a way that the king would be aware of it. Tristan and Andret were the guardians of the queen's chamber. But Tristan did not notice that Andret had made such an arrangement for him.

King Mark was ill and lying in another chamber. That night, when Tristan knew that Andret was asleep, he rose quietly and went to the queen's bed and struck against the scythes and gave himself a great wound in the leg. And it began to bleed very hard, but he lay beside the queen and took no notice of it. The queen, who felt the wet sheets, thought that Tristan was wounded.

"Ah, Tristan," she said, "go back to your bed, for I know that we are being spied upon."

And Tristan left so quietly that Andret never noticed it. And he bound up his wound. And the queen got out of her bed and struck against the scythes, so that she was wounded. And then she shouted,

"Help! Help! Brangien, I'm hurt!"

The damsels came forth and lit the torches, and they found the scythes and said that they had been put there after they were asleep.

"Tristan and Andret, you are the guardians of the chamber. Do you wish the death of my lady? May the king be shamed if he does not have you destroyed!"

Tristan said that he knew nothing of this and so did Andret. The king came and asked Isolt who had done this to her.

"Sire, I know not, but I know full well that Tristan or Andret wishes to kill me, and I pray that you avenge me for it."

And the king pretended to be angry about it.

"Sire," said Tristan, "if you were to say that it was one of us, I would say that it was not done by me, and if Andret denied that it was by him, I would kill or vanquish him."

When King Mark saw that Tristan wished to take it up with Andret, who had done this on his advice, he said,

"Tristan, war between you two would not be proper. Now let us leave it at that, for we shall soon know the truth of this."

Thus was done the treacherous deed of the scythes. Isolt was ill a long time from this wound and Andret was well aware that

43

Tristan had been wounded by the scythes, and he saw to it that the king knew it. And [the king] hated Tristan more than before, and he prayed Andret to work to catch him with the queen.

"For if we could catch him there, I would destroy him."

"Sire," said Andret, "I shall tell you how he will be caught. Forbid him to enter the queen's chamber at night, and in this way he will soon be caught...."

> [*Andret fails in a subsequent attempt to trap Tristan in Isolt's room, but Mark, wary, has Isolt shut up in a tower where Tristan cannot get to her. Aided by Brangien he enters the tower in woman's disguise and stays with Isolt three days. He is betrayed to Andret, however, by a damsel formerly spurned by Tristan.*]
> (Loseth, p. 42.)

THE STAKE

Then Andret came to those who hated Tristan and told them. And they said that they were all prepared, and when this was done Andret told the damsel to come seek him at the right moment. Fifty knights went off with Andret to the tower and entered by the gate. And the damsel came to Andret and said,

"Lord, come, for Tristan is asleep with the queen."

"Lords," said Andret, "since he is asleep he cannot escape you."

Then they lit great torches of wax and went up and went to the queen's bed, and they found Tristan asleep there in his breeches and shirt. Then one of the knights said to Andret,

"Do you want me to kill him in his sleep?"

"No," said Andret, "for the king wants him to be brought back to him alive."

Then they seized him and tied his hands and feet and said,

"Tristan, you are caught. You will be put to shame and the queen destroyed because of this."

When Tristan saw that he was caught and betrayed in this way he was very sorrowful. And they said that they would return him

44

to the king the next day and Isolt also. Isolt wept most piteously and Tristan was most marvelously angry.

The next day Andret came to the king and said to him,

"Sire, we have taken Tristan with Isolt."

"How did you find him?" asked the king. And Andret told him.

"In the name of God," said the king, "the shame is mine. May I never more wear a crown if I do not take my vengeance of this. Go and have them brought to me."

And he did so. When Tristan's four companions[7] heard this news, they came to Gouvernal and told him what had happened to Tristan. Gouvernal was greatly sorrowed to hear it. Then they decided to place themselves in ambush in some thickets that were near the place where criminals were executed. And if Tristan were taken there they would rescue him or die. Then they armed themselves and, along with Gouvernal, went off and placed themselves in ambush in the thickets. Tristan and the queen were brought before the king.

"Tristan," said the king, "I sought your honor and you my shame. If I dishonor you, none should blame me for it. And I shall do you such dishonor that never again will you do ill to me or another."

Then the king ordered a fire to be built at the seashore and that they be burned in it.

"Ah, sire," said those of Cornwall, "avenge yourself on the queen in another way than by burning her! Deliver her to the lepers. With them she will suffer greater torment than if she were burned. And let Tristan be burned."

And the king said that this was most agreeable to him. The fire was built near the place where the four companions were. The king gave the order to Andret that Tristan be burned and that the queen be delivered to the lepers, and he said that he would do so willingly. Then he handed Tristan over to ten menials and Isolt to ten others.

7. Lambegues, Drians, Fergus, and Nicorant. See Löseth, p. 38.

45

When the king saw Tristan and Isolt being led away, he was so sorrowful that he could not look at them, and he went into his chamber, lamenting in his grief, and he said,

"Now I am the vilest king and the basest that ever was, when I order the destruction in such a way of Tristan, my nephew, who had surpassed everyone in the world in chivalry, and of my wife who surpassed in beauty all on earth."

Then he cursed Andret and all those who had given him this counsel, for he would rather have kept her than give her to the lepers. Thus did the king lament against those who were taking Tristan and Isolt away.

When the people saw Tristan being led to his death, they said,

"Ah, Tristan! If the king were to recall the anguish you suffered from your encounter with the Morholt for the liberation of Cornwall, he would not have you put to death but would honor you and hold you dear."

Tristan was led along until he came to an old church that was situated on the shore. Tristan looked at it and said that if he were inside it God would send him some counsel. Then he worked until he loosened and broke his bonds and the ropes that he was bound with. And he leaped upon one of the menials, who was holding him and who had a sword. And he took it from him and cut off his head, and he fell dead. And when the others saw Tristan untied and holding the sword, they dared stay no longer, but turned in flight and left him. And Tristan leaped into the church and went up to a window looking out on the sea and saw that the sea was a good forty fathoms deep there. Then he said that he would have none of the wretched knights of Cornwall, for he would rather let himself fall into the sea than die at their hands. Then Andret arrived, and with him a good twenty knights, and said,

"Ah, Tristan, that does you no good, for you cannot escape."

"Certainly, you brigand," said Tristan, "if I die it will not be at the hands of such vile folk as you. I would rather throw myself into this sea."

Then they came at him, bare swords in hand. And Tristan hit

one and struck him dead. And the others came at him from all directions. Tristan saw that he could not hold out, for he was bare of armor and they were in armor, and he cast himself into the sea from one of the windows. When they saw this, they said that he was surely drowned. This leap must indeed be called Tristan's Leap.

Then they went on to a house of lepers, and the queen said to Andret,

"Ah, for God's sake, kill me before you deliver me to such vile folk, or lend me your sword and I shall kill myself!"

"Lady," said Andret, "you must remain here."

And the lepers then seized Isolt and led her off by force. And Andret then departed. One of the queen's damsels was there. When she saw that her lady had been delivered to the lepers, she fled in mortal fear straight to the thickets where the four companions and Gouvernal were. When Gouvernal saw her coming, he said,

"Lady, have no fear."

And she, recognizing Gouvernal, was reassured and she said,

"Ah, Gouvernal, my lady has been delivered to the lepers. For God's sake, save her!"

"And of Tristan," he asked, "have you any news?"

"Truly, none."

When the four companions heard the news of the queen, they said to Gouvernal,

"Go straightway and save the queen."

"Willingly," said Gouvernal.

"Damsel," he said, "take me to where she is."

And the damsel led them to the place. Gouvernal took the queen and placed her before him and led her back to the thicket with the four companions.

"Lady," said the companions, "can you tell us news of Tristan?"

"Certainly," she said, "I saw him go into an old church, and I think he may be drowned."

47

When they heard this, they began to lament most sorrowfully.

"For God's sake," said Gouvernal, "let us see whether we can find the body, and we will take it to the household of King Arthur, before the Round Table. For such was often his request, that, in the event of his death, he be taken there."

And they said that they would do so willingly.

"Now I shall tell you," said Gouvernal, "what we will do. Lambegues and Drians will remain here to guard the queen. And I, Fergus, and Nicorant will go to the chapel to look for Tristan."

With these words they were all in agreement. Then they went off to the chapel and the other two remained with Queen Isolt.

When they arrived at the chapel, they looked out of the window from which Tristan had leaped, and they saw how high it was and how marvelously deep was the sea, and they said that in no way could anyone escape who jumped from here. Then they looked around, and they saw Tristan sitting on a little rock, in his hand the sword that he had taken from the menial.

"In God's name," said Fergus, "I see Tristan safe and sound!"

"By all that I hold dear," said Nicorant, "so do I! How can we get him? We cannot reach him, nor he us, except by sea." Then Fergus cried out and said,

"Sire, how shall we get to you?"

When Tristan saw them, he was overjoyed, and he pointed to them to go to the right, toward the rock. And he began to swim and reached his companions. Then they dismounted and kissed and embraced him and asked how it was with him.

"I am well," he said, "thanks to God. But tell me news of Isolt."

"Certainly," they said, "we shall return her to you safe and sound."

"Certainly," said Tristan, "since I shall have her I suffer no pain."

Then Tristan mounted Gouvernal's horse and Gouvernal mounted behind one of the companions, and they rode until they came to where Isolt was, who was grieving most sorrowfully for Tristan, for she thought that she had indeed lost him. And when she saw him there was no question of her joy. The queen asked Tristan whether he was well and happy.

"Lady," said Tristan, "yes, thanks to God, when I see you well and happy. Henceforth nothing could grieve me. And since God has united us, we shall never leave each other."

"Certainly," said Isolt, "this pleases me, for I would rather be poor with you than rich without you."

Great was their joy because God had brought them together. And so Tristan and Isolt escaped death.

THE FOREST OF MOROIS

"Tell me," said Tristan to his companions, "do you know where we can find shelter today?"

"Yes," they said, "there is the house of a forester near here. If we can reach it, he will willingly give us shelter."

"That is true," said Tristan, "I know him well."

Then they mounted and went off to the house of the forester, who welcomed them most hospitably. And as soon as he heard Tristan, who had done him many kindnesses, he showed great joy, and he said,

"Lord, I am yours entirely, and whatever I have, and I shall serve you in spite of all those in Cornwall who wished to put you to death."

"Now do not be concerned," said Tristan, "they would now willingly repent of this, if they could. And you may be sure that I shall not leave here until I have avenged myself on them."

That night they were most richly served. The forester gave garments to Tristan and robes and palfreys to Isolt, for which Tristan was most grateful to him.

And know that the forest where they were was called the forest of Morois and was the biggest forest in Cornwall. When they had been in that place as long as it pleased Tristan, they took leave and departed. Tristan rode along all lost in thought. And when he had reflected, he said to Queen Isolt,

49

"Lady, what shall we do? If I take you to the kingdom of Logres, I shall be called a traitor and you a disloyal queen. And if I take you to Lyonesse, everyone will blame me and say that I am keeping the wife of my uncle."

"Tristan," said Isolt, "do according to your will, for I shall do whatever pleases you."

"Lady," said Tristan, "I shall tell you. Near here there is a manor which belonged to the Wise Damsel, and if we were there, I and you, Gouvernal, and your damsel, we would have no concern that anyone might take our joy from us there. And when we had been there a year or two, God would send us some counsel."

"Ah, Tristan!" said Isolt, "then we shall be lost here, for we shall see no one—neither knight, nor lady, nor damsel, nor any other."

"Certainly," said Tristan, "since I see you, I desire never to see any lady, damsel, or any person other than you. And for you I am willing to leave the whole world and have us dwell in this forest."

"Sire," said Isolt, "I shall do as you command."

[*Tristan sends his four companions off.*] (*Loseth, p. 43.*)

Tristan, Gouvernal, Isolt, and her damsel rode on until they came to the castle of which they had spoken earlier. This castle was most fair. And a youth of Cornwall had had it built for a damsel whom he loved, and there they lived until their death. The damsel was very learned in enchantments. When those who loved her sought her and came before the castle, they could see neither the castle nor [the two lovers], and yet they could speak to them.

When Tristan and Isolt arrived there, Tristan asked Isolt how the place seemed to her.

"Certainly," said Isolt, "it is fair. I never want to leave it."

"Certainly, lady," said Tristan, "it is lovely here, for here are the fountains, and every day we shall have plenty of venison. And Gouvernal will go get other things for us."

50

Thus did Tristan dwell in the forest of Morois, he and Isolt, Gouvernal, and the damsel, who was called Lamide. Tristan said to Gouvernal that if he could have Passebreul, his horse, and Hudein, his dog, he would ask for no more.

"In the name of God," said Gouvernal, "I shall go to King Mark and tell him to send them to you."

"Go quickly," said Tristan.

Gouvernal mounted his horse and rode off until he came to Norhoult, where he found King Mark in great anger because Tristan and Isolt had escaped from him. For he feared Tristan greatly, and those of Cornwall did also, since they knew full well that Tristan would not hold one of them in his power whom he would not put to death. When Gouvernal had come before the king, he said to him without greeting,

"King Mark, Tristan sends word that you send him Passebreul, his horse, and Hudein, his dog."

And the king answered,

"Willingly."

And he had them given to him. And then he asked where Tristan was. And Gouvernal said that he would not tell him. Then Gouvernal left the king and traveled until he came back to his lord Tristan. When Tristan saw him he was overjoyed.

Tristan began to hunt and put his mind to killing animals. Thus did Tristan take delight in the hunt and in the company of Isolt, and he spent his life in such fashion that he no longer remembered anyone. There Tristan taught Hudein, his dog, to hunt without barking, so that he should in no way be spied out. King Mark knew full well that Tristan was in the forest of Morois, but he did not know where. And therefore he dared not go into the forest unless he had with him at least twenty armed knights.

One day it happened that King Mark was riding in the forest of Morois with a great company of men, and he was saying that if he did not have Isolt he would die. And he said that he would have given half of his kingdom for her to be with him, so that he might never lose her. And it happened that he found four shepherd boys by a fountain, and he asked them whether they knew any news of a man who lived in the forest, who rode a big sorrel horse. And the youths, who meant no harm, said,

"Sire, are you asking for Tristan, King Mark's nephew?"

"Yes," said the king.

"He lives in the house of the Wise Damsel," they said, "and he has with him a lady and a damsel and a squire."

And the king asked his men if there were any among them who knew the manor.

"Sire," they said, "yes."

"Let us go there," said the king.

Then they went off to the spot. And Tristan was not there at that moment, nor Gouvernal. The king ordered them to go in and bring Isolt to him, and, if Tristan tried to defend her, to kill him. They went in, and they found Isolt all alone except for a damsel. And they took them and brought them before the king. And Isolt cried out,

"Ah, Tristan! Help! Help!"

"Lady, Tristan can help you no more."

Then they delivered her to the king. And when the king had her, he said,

"Let us go from here, for I have indeed come upon what I was seeking. Now let Tristan seek another Isolt, for this one he shall not have!"

Then they turned back and rode until they came to Norhoult. The king had Isolt dressed as finely as he could and had her put in his tower. And he flattered and spoke soft words to her with all his might. But it was of no avail, for if he had given her the whole world she would have had no joy, since she did not have Tristan.

Then the king had it announced throughout Cornwall that to whoever would bring him Tristan, dead or alive, he would give the best city in Cornwall. After this proclamation, those of Cornwall assembled, here twenty, there thirty, elsewhere forty, to look for Tristan. And they said that he had with him only Gouvernal. Tristan knew full well that they were seeking him and would willingly have met them, if he had been well. But it happened that, on the day he lost Isolt, he was sleeping by a hedge, and Gouvernal was not with him where he was asleep. There came a youth carrying a bow and arrows. When he saw Tristan, he recognized him and said,

"Tristan, you killed my father, but I shall avenge him, if I can, right now."

Then he said that if he killed him in his sleep it would be treachery. Then he said that he would wake him and on his awaking would strike him with two or three arrows. Then he cried out,

"Tristan, you are dead!"

Tristan awoke and leaped up as soon as he heard himself thus called. And as he rose the other struck him with a poisoned arrow. And Tristan rushed upon him and seized him by the arm and struck him against a rock, so that he dashed his brains out completely. And then he took the arrow out of his arm and thought that no harm was done. But he had not gone very far when he saw that his arm was all swollen. Then he knew full well that the arrow had been poisoned. But it did not matter to him, for Isolt, whom he thought he would find, would soon have him cured of it.

Then he came to where he had left Gouvernal and told him his adventure. And they mounted and rode until they came to their dwelling. And then they entered and found no one.

"Ah, God!" said Tristan, "I have lost Isolt. The king has surely taken her off. Certainly now I would wish to die, for never shall I have joy."

Then they went looking everywhere, but they found nothing, and they were all griefstricken. Tristan was so disconsolate that he said that, if he were not deterred, he would kill himself, for he had indeed deserved death when he had left Isolt all alone without a guard.

That night he spent in sorrow. The next day, as soon as it was light, Tristan looked at his arm, which was bigger around than his thigh, and he was completely terror-stricken at it.

"Sire," said Gouvernal, "you are in peril of death if you do not receive counsel quickly."

"Certainly," said Tristan, "I do not know where I may get it, since I have lost Isolt."

"In the name of God," said Gouvernal, "if you wish it, I shall go and speak to her."

"Yes," said Tristan, "and I shall accompany you to the edge of the forest."

Then they mounted and rode to the edge of the forest, and they found a damsel who belonged to Isolt and was related to Brangien. Tristan greeted her, and when she recognized him she began to weep. And he asked her for news of Isolt. And she told him that the king had shut her up in his tower where she had been formerly, so that none could speak to her.

"Ah, God!" said Tristan, "and what shall I do? I am wounded, as you see, and I do not know who might counsel me."

"Certainly, sire, I do not know, for you have failed Isolt. But if you can speak to Brangien, she will counsel you well. Wait for me and I shall send her here to you."

"Ah," said Tristan, "much thanks!"

Then the damsel left Tristan and went on until she came to court, and she told Brangien the message that Tristan had given her. When Brangien heard this, she mounted and left the court and came to Tristan. They received Brangien in great joy.

ISOLT OF THE WHITE HANDS

And when she saw Tristan so sorely wounded, she said,

"Ah, sire, you are dead if you do not have counsel. And this may not be here, for you have failed my lady."

"Ah, God!" said Tristan, "and I shall die then for so little cause?"

"Not at all," said Brangien. "I shall tell you what to do. You will go to Brittany and to the dwelling of King Hoel, who has a daughter named Isolt of the White Hands. She is so learned in medicine that she will soon have you cured."

When Tristan heard the name Isolt, he was so joyous that it seemed to him that he was already cured.

"Brangien," he said, "since you advise me to do this, I shall go there. Now I pray that you greet my lady for me when you see her and tell her that I am Tristan the Sickly." Then they parted from each other in great sorrow.

Tristan rode on until he came to Brittany, to a castle that was called Habugue. There he found King Hoel, who was having the gates of the castle shut on account of a neighbor who was making war on him, named Agrippes. Tristan found the king before his gate and greeted him, and the king him. The king asked who he was.

"Sire," he said, "I am a strange knight, ill and sorely wounded. And I have been told that you have a daughter who would soon have me cured, if she were willing."

The king looked at Tristan, who would have been most fair, had he been in good health, and well formed. And he thought that if he were well he would be a most noble man. And he said to Tristan,

"Certainly, sir knight, I do not know who you are. But I shall willingly hand you over to my daughter for healing, and I shall pray her to take pains to cure you."

"Sire, thanks to you," said Tristan.

Then the king went and had his daughter come, and he said to her,

"Daughter, here is a strange knight who is ill. I pray you take pains to cure him as you would me, myself."

"Sire," she said, "most willingly, since it pleases you."

Then she took Tristan and led him to her chamber. And when she saw the arm, she said that there was poison in it.

"But do not be dismayed, for I shall cure you completely and soon, if it please God."

Then she sought and put on his wound what she knew he needed, until Tristan was cured. And he improved greatly in a short time and came back to his beauty and his strength.

Tristan looked at Isolt and loved her sorely. And he thought that if he could have her, he would take her willingly and so would forget the other Isolt. Tristan was certain that he could forget the other Isolt for many reasons, for he saw full well that he held her against right and against reason. And there was no one, if he were to learn of it, who would not hold him for a wicked man and a traitor. Therefore he decided that it would be better for him to take this Isolt and leave the other Isolt. Isolt, who was unaware of this, took such pains and such care of Tristan that he was cured. And when he saw that he could bear arms, he was overjoyed and frolicked and laughed. And everyone who saw him said,

"Certainly, if he is not a noble man he must indeed hate his fair form."

For he was so fair in all beauty that Isolt, who had never been in love, became quite mad about him, so that she thought of nothing but him.

KEHEDIN

Isolt had a brother, a fair knight, noble and vigorous, who was named Kehedin.[8] In all of Brittany there was no knight of such great renown as his. Now he was waging the war more than his father, and had he not done so the war would soon have been ended. After Tristan was cured, King Hoel met Count Agrippes in battle. But the king was defeated and lost a great number of men and knights. And Kehedin was wounded, so that they thought him mortally wounded, and he was brought back on his shield. And the king had the gates shut. Isolt saw her wounded brother, and she labored hard to heal him. Count Agrippes besieged the town and ordered ten battalions, in each five hundred men. The first two battalions went off toward the citadel, and the other eight were placed in a wood nearby.

Those of the citadel shut the gates and went up on the battle-

8. A variant spelling, in MS. 103, is Kaherdin.

ments to defend it. The king came to his son and began to weep and said,

"Ah, son! If the count did not know that you were wounded, he would not have undertaken this today! Fair son, you were my hope to put an end to my war, but since I have lost you, I am sure to lose my land."

When Gouvernal saw the king's sorrow, he said,

"Ah, king, do not be afflicted, for God will send you help. You have here the best knight in the world."

"What!" said the king, "I do not think that there is in this country a knight as good as Kehedin, my son."

"Faith," said Gouvernal, "there is one better by half."

"Ah," said the king, "for God's sake, tell me who he is!"

"I shall tell you," said Gouvernal, "provided the thing be kept secret."

"Certainly," said the king, "I promise you that it shall never be revealed by me."

"Certainly, sire," said Gouvernal, "it is the knight to whom I belong. I shall not tell you his name, but this much I will tell you in truth, that he is the best knight in the world. And if he were outside, with very little help he would soon bring to defeat those who go against you."

"Ah, God!" said the king, "then I am delivered, since I have here such a knight! Certainly I shall request his help."

"Sire," said Gouvernal, "he will indeed not fail you if you request it of him."

Then he asked where the strange knight was. And they told him that he had gone up on the walls.

"Go seek him for me at once," said the king, and they did so. And Tristan, who was looking at those of the citadel, who dared not go forth, was very angry.

"Ah, God!" he said, "it has been so long since I have borne arms! I have indeed wasted my time for love of Isolt, and Isolt has done so for love of me!..."

[*Tristan dons his armor, goes down to the battlefield, and accomplishes marvels of prowess in defeating and killing Agrippes. King Hoel recovers his land.*] (*Loseth, p. 45.*)

After this defeat they were in a great turmoil to know who Tristan was and his name. When Isolt of the White Hands heard him praised thus, if she had loved him before, she loved him henceforth a hundred times more. And it moved her that he willingly took his leisure with her, so that she thought that he loved her. And so did he, in part for her beauty and in part for her name.

One day it happened that King Hoel was seated at table at mealtime, and he saw Tristan in a gayer humor than he had ever seen, and he said to him,

"Sire, if it pleased you, you would tell me your name, for all those here desire greatly to know it."

Tristan began to smile and said,

"Sire, my name is Tristan, and I was born in Lyonesse, a man of poor worth and little renown."

Kehedin was already well, and he honored Tristan greatly for his good chivalry. One day Tristan and Kehedin were riding together. Tristan began to think of Queen Isolt, so that he did not know whether he was asleep or awake. Kehedin took good note of this but said not a word. So lost was he in thought that he heaved a great sigh and then said,

"Ah, fair Isolt, you have killed me!"

Then he fell off his horse to the ground all in a faint. And then he came to his senses, as though he were waking from sleep, and he was all ashamed because of Kehedin. And Kehedin said to him,

"Sire, it is not good sense to think too much."

"You speak truly," said Tristan, "but in the case of a man whose heart rules him, it is no wonder if he goes astray at times."

"Sire," said Kehedin, "I see you lost in thought more than I would like, and indeed I believe that it is on account of a lady or damsel. And if it pleased you to tell me, I promise you certainly that I would do all in my power, were I to die for it, to do your pleasure."

"Certainly," said Tristan, "I shall tell you. I love Isolt so that I am languishing and dying on account of it, as you can see. And if there were no Isolt, I would not be in this land. And if you would give me Isolt, I would be most happy."

When Kehedin heard this, he became overjoyed, for he thought that it was Isolt, his sister, of whom he was speaking, for he had never heard of any other Isolt, and he would willingly have him take her to wife. For he was such a valiant knight that she would be very well married to him, and all of Brittany would be honored in it. So he said to him,

"Tristan, why have you kept this secret from me for so long? Know that if I had thought that you wanted to have her, you would never have suffered such pain for it. And I shall willingly give her to you as soon as we are at court."

Tristan, who saw that Kehedin wished to give him the Isolt about whom he was not thinking, decided not to refuse her, because he had asked for Isolt and because he would not reveal himself further, and he thanked him. Then they turned back and went on until they came to court. Kehedin came to his father and told him how Tristan loved Isolt. When the king heard this news, he was overcome with joy and said,

"I shall not only give him Isolt, but I shall give him myself and you and all of Brittany in its entirety with Isolt. And if all the world were mine, I would give it to him, for he is indeed worthy of it."

Then he sent for Isolt, his daughter, and gave her to Tristan. And Tristan took her most joyfully. And know that if the other Isolt loved him, this Isolt loved him two hundredfold more.

THE MARRIAGE OF TRISTAN

Tristan wedded Isolt. And great were the wedding festivities and the celebration. And night came, when Tristan was to lie with

Isolt. But the other Isolt forbade him to lie with his wife carnally, but embracing and kissing she did not forbid. Tristan lay down by Isolt, all bare flesh to bare flesh, and the light shone so bright that Tristan could clearly see Isolt's beauty. Her throat was soft and white, her eyes changing in color and laughing, her brows brown and comely, her face pure and bright. And Tristan kissed and embraced her. And when he remembered Isolt of Cornwall, he indeed lost his will to do more. This Isolt was before him, and the other Isolt was in Cornwall, forbidding him, for as dear as he held himself, to do anything to this one which would turn out basely. Thus did Tristan remain with Isolt, his wife. And she, who knew nothing of any solace other than embracing and kissing, fell asleep in Tristan's arms, until the next morning when the ladies and damsels came to see Tristan and Isolt.

Tristan rose and then went off to the palace. When the king saw him, he came up to him and said,

"Friend Tristan, you have accomplished so much that you have earned the kingdom of Brittany. Here, I give it to you and endow you with it, in the sight of all those who are here."

And Tristan received it and thanked him greatly for it. Gouvernal was overjoyed at this, for he thought that this Isolt would make him forget the other Isolt and that he had lain carnally with this one. What shall I tell you? Isolt loved Tristan with all her heart, and Tristan loved her for her name and for her beauty. And when Isolt was asked how she loved Tristan, she answered that she loved him more than the whole world. And therefore it was thought certainly that he had lain with her carnally. In this fashion Tristan remained with Isolt nearly a year. Now the tale ceases telling of Tristan and Isolt of the White Hands and returns to tell of Isolt of Cornwall—how she behaved when the king had her taken from Tristan.

Now the tale tells that when King Mark had regained Isolt and had put her in his tower, and she saw that she had lost Tristan whom she loved more than anything living in the whole world, she was so sorrowful that she began to weep most sorely and cursed the hour and the day she was born. She wasted away so sorely on account of the great sorrow she was suffering that all who saw her marveled. King Mark, who loved her more than himself, was so distraught that he did not know what to do. He cajoled her as best he could to make her forget her grief, but it was of no avail. Since she did not have Tristan, nothing could comfort her. He was her death, he was her life, he was her joy and her health. She said that she would never have joy nor anything good, since she had lost Tristan. Brangien, who loved her greatly, comforted her and said,

"Lady, for God's sake, have pity on yourself. Do not kill yourself in this way. Know that he will not delay long in coming back. Know that if the whole world forbade him to come back he would come. And, once returned, you would find some counsel whereby you could speak together."

Thus Brangien comforted Isolt.

And it happened that news came one day to Cornwall that Tristan had married Isolt of the White Hands. At this King Mark was overjoyed, for he thought surely that Tristan would never return to Cornwall. Queen Isolt, who had heard this news, was so griefstricken at it that she almost went out of her mind. This news was her death sentence. There was none who could comfort her. She said that she would kill herself. Then she recalled Brangien and said to her,

"Ah, Brangien! Have you heard about Tristan, whom I loved so and and more than all the world, who has thus betrayed me? Ah, Tristan! Tristan! Tristan! Where have you taken the heart to betray the one who loved you more than herself? Ah treacherous, disloyal, and false Love! Ill do you know how to reward for their service those who serve you! And since it is thus that I see all have joy of their love, and I am all wretched and sorrowful and in pain on account of it, I pray God that he quickly send me death...."

[*Brangien advises her to write Queen Guinevere a letter complaining of love and Tristan.*] (*Bédier, II, 370.*)

In this part the tale tells that Tristan and Kehedin were riding together one day, and Tristan remembered that it was a year since he had lost Isolt, and he began to weep most sorely. When Kehedin saw him weeping, he knew surely that it was out of great distress at heart and he said to him,

"Sire, by the faith you owe to what you love most in the world, tell me why you are weeping."

"Kehedin," said Tristan, "you have long entreated me, but if you promise me to tell no one and not to bear me ill will for it, I shall tell you."

And Kehedin promised this to him loyally.

"Kehedin," said Tristan, "I love a lady who was taken from me a year ago today."

And then he told him the truth of his love.

"And know," said Tristan, "that I can indeed return your sister to you still a maid, for I love Isolt so that I would never do her wrong for anything."

"Sire," said Kehedin, "I marvel greatly at what you tell me, and nevertheless I do indeed believe you. But now tell me. Is the lady you love beautiful?"

"Of her beauty," said Tristan, "there is no need to talk, for in all the world there is none so fair, and never did woman love man as she loves me."

"Certainly," said Kehedin, "if she is so fair and she loves you as much as you say, I shall never blame you if you love her. Now tell me what counsel you wish to take to relieve this pain."

"I will tell you," said Tristan. "I shall go to her and take her away to the kingdom of Logres or to Lyonesse, and then we shall spend our lives in joy."

"Certainly," said Kehedin, "I advise it, and better is it for you to have the one from whom you cannot free yourself and for you to live with her in joy than with my sister in sorrow. And, if it pleased you, I would go with you to comfort you and to see the lady."

And Tristan granted this to him.

[*Numerous adventures take place before their departure.*] (*Loseth, pp. 46, 48–51, 60.*)

Then they put to sea and on the third day they arrived close by
Tintagel. Then they put on their armor and mounted.

"Brangien," [9] said Tristan, "where shall we go?"

"Sire," she said, "we shall go to a castle near here which belongs
to Dynas, who will receive us most joyfully if we find him."

Then they journeyed on until they came to the castle. Tristan
went into the garden, and Brangien went ahead and found Dynas,
who was overjoyed at her coming and asked her if she knew any
news of Tristan.

"Would you be happy to see him?" she asked.

"Certainly, yes," he said, "for he is the knight I love most in all
the world."

"Would you want him to be in this castle?" asked Brangien.

"May God help me," said Dynas, "if he were here and King
Mark were outside with an army, I would rather die than that
Tristan should come to harm."

"Then know," said Brangien, "that he is in this castle."

"Ah, for God's sake!" said Dynas, "take me to him!"

Then she took him to the garden where Tristan was. When
Dynas saw Tristan, he ran to embrace and kiss him, and he took
him to his tower and said to him,

"Tristan, you may stay here as long as it pleases you, for I place
in your hands myself and whatever I have."

"Dynas," said Tristan, "much thanks. Much honor have you
done me. Now I should like my lady to know that I am here."

"Sire," said Dynas, "you will stay here and I and Kehedin shall
go to court, and I shall speak to my lady, the queen."

"You speak rightly," said Tristan.

The next day Dynas and Kehedin went to court. King Mark
received Kehedin most honorably, for he thought that he was a
knight errant. And as soon as Kehedin saw Isolt, he loved her so

9. For the details of how Brangien joins them, see Bédier, II, 269–72.

sorely that never afterward did his heart leave her until death. And
Dynas told the queen that Tristan had come. And know that she
was overjoyed at this....

> [*Tristan and Kehedin manage to rejoin Isolt and*
> *Brangien in Cornwall. After various ruses and*
> *adventures, Tristan is discovered. He escapes and goes*
> *back to Brittany. (Bédier, II, 269–70.) Kehedin's*
> *brother, Ruvalen, confides in Tristan concerning his*
> *love of Gargeolain, wife of Bedalis.] (Bédier, II,*
> *282; Loseth, p. 37.)*

But now the tale ceases telling of this matter and speaks of
Tristan, who had come back to Karahes in Brittany with King
Hoel and Isolt of the White Hands, his wife, and Ruvalen, who
was King Hoel's son and brother to Kehedin and Isolt, Tristan's
wife. [They] prepared great festivities and a joyous celebration for
Tristan, and all those of the country did also, when he was back in
Karahes. Now the tale tells that Tristan and Ruvalen were to-
gether one day, and Tristan said,

"Fair sweet friend, I marvel greatly that you tell me no news of
Gargeolain, your beloved."

"Faith," said Ruvalen, all smiles, "I have never yet spoken to
her except one single time, and even then it was on the parapet of
the moat at her manor. And she was shut up inside, and I was
outside. For Bedalis, her baron, who is so jealous of her, had taken
away the key to the gate. And she told me this much, when I spoke
to her, that she would send me the impressions of all the keys to the
place in wax, if I desired. And I wonder greatly that I have heard
no news of her."

"Faith," said Tristan, "it would be a good thing if you had the
impressions. And I know a smith in Nantes, who came from
Nicole for love of me, who will fashion them according to the
model better and more properly than anyone else."

When they had spoken at length of their purpose, they departed
from there, and they devised such a plan which was later the cause

of their death in great sorrow. And because of it Tristan lost the quest of the Holy Grail on which he had embarked with the other companions of the Round Table.

One day Tristan and Ruvalen had gone hunting in the forest. Now there came to them Cadio, Gargeolain's messenger, with a tightly shut box on which there were wax seals. When Cadio saw Ruvalen he came to him and drew the box from his bosom and said,

"Sire, your beloved Gargeolain greets you and sends you this box. And know that there is no key the impression of which is not here. Now tell me your will, for I wish to depart hence yet tonight."

"Friend," said Ruvalen, "you shall greet her for me and tell her that I am hers entirely."

Then Cadio departed and Tristan came spurring up to Ruvalen, horn around his neck, and saw the box he was holding in his hand. And he knew full well that Gargeolain had sent it to him, and he said to him,

"Ruvalen, not everyone knows what there is inside this box."

Then he took it from Ruvalen's hand and broke the lock and saw inside it his great sorrow and his death and his harm. But he was not aware of it.

When Tristan and Ruvalen saw the seals, they were overjoyed at what was to do them harm. But it is said that one is at times more bound to one's ill than to one's good, and one goes more willingly to where one has torment than one does to where one has joy and delight. All this I have said relating to Tristan and to Ruvalen, who were overjoyed at the seals which were the cause of their death. But they were not aware of it. Tristan hunted the whole day and so did Ruvalen, and they took an animal that they carried back to Karahes. It was time for supper, so they ate and went to sleep and rest from the pains they had taken on the hunt. The next morning Tristan sent word to Nantes for Goudri, the smith, to come speak to him, and he came. Tristan took him in all secrecy to a chamber away from everything and said to him,

"Goudri, fair friend, I have great trust in you, and I have sent for you for a matter of great need to me. Girolebours, who holds a castle from me, does not deign to serve me or do what he owes me. And the watch of the castle have sent me here the seals of all the gates of the towers and the fortified places. And therefore I pray you to fashion the keys according to the model of the seals and that there be neither more nor fewer, and that I may have them within a week. And take care that this secret be revealed to no one."

"Sire," said Goudri, "do not worry nor be dismayed, for no one in the world shall ever know it through me."

Then Goudri, the smith, departed and took along the impressions of the keys, and he began to fashion them, and he made the keys well and fairly, so that there were neither more nor fewer than those for which he had the impressions on the seals. Ah, if they had known what an evil fashioning this was! But they were not aware of it, and so there was great sorrow and harm to all of chivalry. But now the tale ceases speaking of Goudri and the keys and speaks of Count Urnoy of Nantes who was beginning a revolt against Tristan.

In this part the tale tells that when King Hoel of Karahes died, Urnoy, Count of Nantes, whom Tristan had already taken before the gates of Karahes, and the barons of the land, began to revolt against Tristan and Ruvalen. One day Tristan was in his hall, where he was playing chess with Isolt, his wife. There came before him a messenger from Urnoy, Count of Nantes, who said to him without greeting,

"Tristan, I defy you on behalf of the Count of Nantes, who sends you word that he is returning to you your truce and your peace and says that he will hold from you neither land nor anything whatever...."

[Tristan, thus challenged, leads an army against the Count of Nantes, takes him prisoner in single combat, and captures the city. But the tower of Nantes resists. During the assault, Tristan is seriously wounded in

the face by a stone thrown at him from the top of the
walls.] (Bédier, II, 374; Loseth, pp. 374–75.)

Tristan came back to Karahes, gravely wounded. And he sent
all around for physicians to cure him. The physicians labored
mightily until he was healed. One day he was lying on his bed,
almost well, and the desire seized him to lie with his wife, and he
lay with her and had his will with her. And when he had done his
desire, he fell down by her all in a faint, as though dead. And when
his wife saw this, she was utterly terrified. And she sent for the
physician, who came very quickly. And when he saw Tristan, he
feared that he was dead, and he was certain that he had lain with
Isolt, his wife, and he said,

"Ah, Tristan, what a misfortune is your death!"

The lady told him to be silent and that there should be no more
of this. The physician made a potion and opened his teeth with a
knife and poured it into him. As soon as Tristan had drunk of it, he
sighed and opened his eyes, and when he saw the physician he was
ashamed. The physician had him borne out of there and set to
work with great effort to cure him. And he took great pains, and
he healed him well and fairly, and Tristan paid him as much as he
wanted, and the physician took leave and went off to his country.
But now the tale ceases speaking of this matter and tells how
Tristan went to see Queen Isolt, his beloved, in Cornwall and how
he played the fool. And here begin straightway Tristan's follies.

TRISTAN THE FOOL

Now the tale tells that Tristan and his nephew were disporting
themselves one day on the shore, and Tristan remembered Queen
Isolt, his beloved, and he said,

"Alas, sweet love! How can I ever speak to you without being
recognized?"

"Ah, sire, for God's sake!" said his nephew. "Do not be dismayed, for we shall speak to her better than we have ever done,

for you look more like a fool to me, because your hair is shorn and because of the wound you received in the face, than any man who exists."

"Are you telling me the truth?" asked Tristan.

"Certainly, sire, I am," said the youth. Then Tristan and his nephew returned to Karahes. The next morning Tristan had a coat cut out of ugly burlap, without stitching or tunic, ill made and ill cut, and he took a hundred sous without anyone's knowledge. And he saw a serf who was carrying a great bludgeon on his shoulder. Tristan came to him and took it from him. Then he went straight off to the shore, all barefoot, bludgeon on shoulder. He looked just like a fool in every way. And he came to the port and found a boat, which belonged to a burgher of Tintagel who wished to return to his country. Tristan took his pence and began to throw them everywhere like a fool. When the sailors saw him, they had him come aboard their boat and he gave them all his pence. The boat sailed off, until they arrived below Tintagel.

King Mark had come to the port for sport and amusement. Tristan, who had taken a cheese from a cask, leaped out of the boat, bludgeon on shoulder. And when the king saw him, he called him, and Tristan rushed at him as though he were quite mad. And the king and all his companions began to flee right back to the castle of Tintagel and there the king shut himself up, on account of the fool, and Tristan remained outside. The king came to the windows of Queen Isolt, and Tristan, who was quite out of his senses for love, took his cheese and began to eat it. And the king called him and said,

"Fool, what do you think of Queen Isolt?"

"Certainly," said the fool, "if I were to lie with her one night, she would restore to me all my wits that I have lost on account of her."

"Fool," said the king, "where were you born?"

"In England," said he.

"And who was your father?"

"An old hack."

68

"And your mother?"

"A ewe. And my father sent me here to get a piece." Then the queen blushed and bowed her head and remembered Tristan.

"Fool," said the king, "who gave you that wound?"

"I got it," said the fool, "in an attack before this tower."

"And have you ever been in a tournament?" asked the king.

"Yes," said the fool, "in Britain and in Cornwall, where I've killed more than a hundred."

And then they all began to laugh, and they said that he was a born fool. The king had him summoned and admitted to the castle and took a great liking to him for the foolish things he said.

One day he came from church and sat down to play chess with a knight, and the queen watched the game. And Tristan began to look at her, all burning with love of her. But she did not recognize him, so she raised her hand and struck him on the neck and said,

"Fool, why are you looking at me that way?"

"Certainly, lady," said Tristan, "I am mad. And know that for the past week I haven't stopped being mad about you. But if the pain were to be justly shared, you would be as mad as I. And I pray you for God's sake and for the love of Tristan, whose heart you have, that you touch me no more, for certainly the potion that you and he drank at sea is not so bitter in your heart as it is in mad Tristan's."

And he said all this in such a low voice that no one heard it, except Queen Isolt. When the queen heard it, she left the game in great anger and went to her room in great wrath. And she called Camille, her damsel. And she came and asked her what was wrong with her that she was so wrathful.

"Certainly," she said, "that fool has made me very angry. He has thrown Tristan up to me. But I shall never have joy in my heart, and indeed I shall know who said these words to him. The king is due to go hunting, and when he has gone and there is no one here, you shall go and get the fool and bring him to me, for I wish to know who said this to him and what is the source of it."

"Lady," said Camille, "willingly."

The king went off to the woods to hunt, and Camille went to get the fool and brought him to the chamber. The queen called him and said,

"Come here, friend. I struck you today in jest. Here, I shall make it up to you."

Then she took him by the hand and sat him down beside her and said,

"Friend, now tell me who told you that Tristan loved me."

"Lady," he said, "you told me."

"And when was this?" she asked.

"Lady," he said, "not a year ago."

"And who are you, then?"

"Lady, I am Tristan."

"Tristan!" she said.

"Truly, lady."

"Faith," said Isolt, "you have lied! You do not resemble him, so get out of here at once! May misfortune come to the assertion of a fool! And certainly you have spoken ill ever to say that you are Tristan!"

When he saw that she was rejecting him so unpleasantly, he put the ring on his finger that she had given him when he had brought her back to King Mark and King Arthur had made peace in the matter, and he had told her never to believe anything said of him before seeing the ring. Tristan showed her the ring and said,

"Certainly, lady, it is most pleasing to me that you have failed to recognize me, for now I believe surely that you have another love than me. And since this is so, much more fairly could you have told me than by rebuffing me that you did not care for me. And I would have gone back to my country and found another love than you. I saw such an hour when you loved me well, but it is woman's custom to change her feelings quickly. She will never love him who loves her well and loyally, but the one who shames her most she will love with all her heart. And certainly I am justly called a fool, when I have gotten myself up as a fool and have left my country and my land, and have gotten myself beaten and insulted by those scoundrels out there, and have eaten in the ashes, and have lain on the bare ground like a dog for love of you, and never once did you look at me or recognize me!"

When Isolt saw the ring and heard him speak thus, she recognized him. Then she embraced and hugged and kissed him more than a hundred times, and he her. Then Tristan told her how he had gotten the wound on account of which she and the others had failed to recognize him, and he told her his adventures. She gave him robes and linen, for other things he would not take. The queen told the porter that for God's sake he should make a bed for the fool in the hall, anywhere at all, where he might sleep at night.

"Lady," he said, "willingly."

And he made him one under the stairs in a corner out of a bit of straw and two sheets that the queen gave him. There lay Tristan day and night, and when the king went hunting, Tristan went and lay with the queen, so that no one knew of it except Camille. Thus was Tristan at Tintagel for two months, and never was he recognized.

One day King Mark was in front of his tower. There came a messenger from King Arthur, who sent word that he should come and speak to him at Cardwell, for he had need of him. And when King Mark heard the summons of King Arthur, his lord, he said that he would willingly go. Then he made ready and equipped himself and went off to court. As soon as he was gone, Tristan went to lie with Queen Isolt. The porter clearly heard him rise from his bed and went quietly to look at the fool's bed, but he did not find him. Then he followed Tristan's footsteps right to Queen Isolt's chamber. Tristan went into the chamber and Camille, who was waiting for him, closed the door after him again, and he went to lie by Queen Isolt. The porter caught sight of him going in and said that he would find out, if he could, what he was looking for in the queen's chamber. Then he looked through a crack in the wall and saw Tristan lying with Queen Isolt. And when he had seen them together, he went back to bed and was certain that it was Tristan. But Tristan was not aware that he had spied on him.

71

The next day the porter told the chamberlains how he had seen the fool lying with the queen, and he said to them,

"You may be certain that he is Tristan."

When the chamberlains heard this, they were very angry and said that they would again that night place good spies in Queen Isolt's chamber in such concealment that the queen would not notice them. When it was night, Tristan went to the queen's room and sat down by her. The chamberlains had placed their spies in the chamber, of which Tristan was unaware.

"Lady," said Tristan to the queen, "I must go, for I have been seen, and you know it to be so. And if the king were to come and seize me, he would put me to death in shame. I saw the porter and the chamberlain yesterday talking together about me."

And when the queen heard Tristan talk of leaving, she began to weep most piteously and said to him,

"Ah, Tristan, fair sweet love, I know truly that I shall never see you again, nor you me, alive. Now I pray you for God's sake and ask you to grant me a boon."

"Certainly, my lady," said Tristan, "willingly. Ask and you shall have it."

"Fair and sweet love," she said, "I ask, if it happens that you die before I do, or if you are mortally ill before I should be, that you have yourself put on a boat and brought here. And see to it that one side of the boat's sail be white and the other side black. And if you are dead or mortally ill, let the black side be placed looking forward. If you are in good health, let the white side be put forward and the black looking back. And exactly the same shall I do of myself if it should happen to me before it does you. And as soon as the boat has come to port, I shall go and see my great misfortune or my great solace. And I shall take you in my arms and kiss you, and never shall I leave you for anyone. And then I shall die, so that we can both be buried together. For since love is so joined in life, it must not be separated in death. And you may be certain that if I die before you I shall do exactly this."

"Certainly, lady," said Tristan, "I grant this."

Thus did they make the pledge to each other. And then they kissed each other and then Tristan took leave of his love, Queen Isolt. And he separated from her in such a pact, for never again did they see each other alive.

When Tristan had taken leave of Isolt, he went off to the seashore and found a merchant from Karahes who knew and loved him dearly, and he went onto his boat. Then they set sail and sailed until they arrived at the port of Karahes. Tristan was received in great joy, for his people were certain that they had lost him. The next morning, when it was light, the spies told the chamberlains that it was Tristan who had played the fool and that he had lain the night with Queen Isolt.

"Ah, God!" they said, "if King Mark, our lord, finds this out, he will destroy and put all of us to death because we have not seized and detained him. Now there is only one thing to do. Let this thing be secret and my lord not find out, for if he knew, he would have us all killed and put to shame."

So they all agreed that they would not tell him and that it would not be revealed by them. But now the tale is silent about this matter and about Queen Isolt and returns to speak of Tristan and of Ruvalen and of Gargeolain, his love.

THE FATAL ADVENTURE

In this part the tale tells that when Tristan left Queen Isolt of Cornwall, his love, wife of King Mark, his uncle, and returned to Karahes, his men and his people greeted him in great festivity, for they were certain that they had lost him. Most welcome was Tristan and most honorably received.

Now it happened that Tristan and Ruvalen were together one day and were speaking to each other of their desires. Now Goudri, the smith, arrived, bringing the keys he had fashioned, and gave them to Tristan. And he tied them all together with a silken cord, and then he said,

"Friend, let us mount and go see Gargeolain, your love."

"Sire," said Ruvalen, "willingly."

Then they mounted two horses and took no arms other than their swords and went off. Ah, God, what a sorrowful adventure happened to them that day! Tristan had on his head a hat of olive leaves, and off he went, all singing and gay and in great delight, he and Ruvalen, to their death. But they were unaware of it.

Bedalis, Gargeolain's husband, had gone hunting that day and with him a good thirty knights, all of whom he had summoned to keep him company. Tristan and Ruvalen came to the manor before the drawbridge, which was locked shut, and Bedalis had taken the keys with him. Tristan dismounted and shoved the key into the lock of the drawbridge, which was fastened with a chain, and he unlocked it and let it down most quietly and softly. And as the drawbridge was being lowered, his hat fell off, whence came misfortune. Then they passed over and unlocked the gate and all the other doors and came to the chamber where Gargeolain was. And the whole chamber was strewn with green, fresh reeds and curtained off with the fairest and richest curtain that ever was, for the whole story of Arthur and of how he had won dominion over the Britons was portrayed on it, and all the seven arts.

When Ruvalen entered the chamber, he fell into the bed with Gargeolain, his love, who loved him dearly. And Tristan went on the other side and left them together and took a handful of reeds and lay back on the grass and began to toss reeds at the curtain so that they stuck in it. Alas, never had he played such a fatal game! But he was unaware of it, for he did it only to amuse himself. Ruvalen and Gargeolain, his love, were in bed, and they took their pleasure and did all that they wished. It was not long before Bedalis had taken a stag, and he began to sound the catch. Tristan heard it. He knew well what this meant, and he said to Ruvalen,

"Let us leave here, friend, for I have heard Bedalis sound the catch."

Then they took their leave and departed. Ah, God, why were they not armed with their armor? For great use could they have made of it at that moment. But they had nothing except their horses and their swords. Tristan and Ruvalen went off, sportive and gay.

Now Bedalis arrived back at his lodging, sounding his horn and making much noise. And he unlocked the drawbridge and saw the hat which had fallen off Tristan, and he was most suspicious. Then he looked all around, but he saw no place where anyone might have crossed over. And he went in and shut all the doors and found his wife, Gargeolain. And he embraced and kissed her still in his boots. And he fell back on the bed and saw the reeds stuck in the curtain, and he began to shake, for he knew full well that these were Tristan's games. Then he stood up and seized Gargeolain, his wife, and drew his sword and told her that by his father's soul he would kill her if she did not tell him the truth.

"For I know full well that Tristan has been here."

"Certainly he was," she said, "he and Ruvalen, who kissed me by force."

And when Bedalis heard this he was more disturbed than before, and he said,

"Ah, wretched creature, there was more! Tell me the truth or I shall kill you. And if you admit the truth to me, I shall forgive you my anger."

"Certainly," she said, "it matters not to me if you kill me, for I would rather die than be in this prison where you have put me. And when you have killed me, it will be said that it was for no crime. But the blame is yours for your jealousy. And certainly I shall tell you the truth, and then do with me as you will. Know that Ruvalen lay with me and did all his will with me. For I could not defend myself against him, for they were two and I am a woman all alone and without any protection."

When Bedalis heard that Ruvalen had seduced his wife, he came to his men and told them and complained about Tristan and Ruvalen who had done him such shame and said that he would never eat again if he did not have revenge for this. And then they mounted as fast as they could and went off after the two companions who were moving gaily along in the depths of the forest. And

75

they had found a hind and her fawns and had rushed after them in order to take them. But they failed, and it was on account of the evil adventure that was to befall them.

Now Bedalis arrived, and his men, all inflamed to do them harm. Tristan saw them coming and placed himself behind a bush, and they passed by. Bedalis came spurring toward Ruvalen, who was all unarmed, and he ran him through with his sword and killed him, but he did not kill him before Ruvalen drew his sword and struck one of Bedalis' men, named Authon, and cut off his head. When Cadio saw Ruvalen, who had cut off his brother Authon's head, he drew his sword and struck Ruvalen and cut off his head, and he, fell to earth, dead. When Tristan saw Ruvalen dead, he leaped from [behind] the bush and drew his sword and struck Cadio and killed him, and then [he struck] another and killed him, and then a third.

Now Bedalis had a spear with a poisoned tip, and he threw it at Tristan, and it struck him in the hip all the way in to the bone, and it cut through the flesh and the bones and the nerves, and the point and a whole piece of the shaft remained in his hip. Ah, God, what great sorrow this was for the whole country! When Tristan saw himself wounded and Ruvalen dead and saw the great number of men that Bedalis had, he turned back and fled straight to Karahes. Bedalis and his men chased him a long time, but they could not catch him, for he was too well mounted, and they turned back. But never again after that hour did they dare to remain or stop in that country.

When Bedalis had killed Ruvalen and wounded Tristan, he said to his men,

"Now let us flee this country, for if Tristan is able to escape, he will shame and destroy us all and deliver us to shame and torture."

Then they departed and put to sea. And they sailed until they arrived at a fair and noble island in the Chausey Isles, shut off by sea and mountains. And the account tells that there were a good seven hundred in that company, and they became outlaws, that is to say, pirates. And no ship whatever bearing cargo could pass by there without being despoiled and its crew put to death and destruction....

THE FATAL ILLNESS

In this part the tale tells that when Bedalis had killed Ruvalen and wounded Tristan, Tristan fled to Karahes, and the blood flowed from him in traces wherever he went. When Tristan entered Karahes, his people saw the blood coming out of him, and they were all astonished and went after him into the castle to learn what was the matter with him. When he came into the castle and dismounted from his horse in great pain and torment, he fell on them, all in a faint, for he had lost too much blood. And when he came to from his faint, he said that Bedalis had killed Ruvalen and wounded him fatally. When Isolt, his wife, and his people heard this, they lamented so, that hardhearted indeed would anyone have been who saw them without being moved to pity. Tristan pointed out to them where they would find Ruvalen dead. Then they mounted and went off, following the trace of blood, and they found Ruvalen dead, his head cut off. Then there began such great grief that Gargeolain heard it in her manor, where she was. And she came out and went to where the crying was, all in a fright. And she found her love dead and was so sorrowful that she fainted over the body more than a hundred times. And when she came from her faint, she said,

"Ah, Ruvalen, noble man, son of a king, you died for me! I shall also die for love of you, and my soul shall keep yours company, and we shall be buried near each other."

With these words she fainted, and her heart burst, and her soul left her body. Then they made a bier of foliage and placed the two bodies on it. And they were all astonished at the adventure, and they carried them in great sorrow to be buried. The archbishop sang mass and put them into the ground one beside the other in two of the richest tombs that were ever again seen. And thus did die Ruvalen and Gargeolain, his love, and were buried together.

77

Tristan sent for physicians from everywhere to heal him from his wound. Among the other physicians there came one whose name was Agar. He removed the shaft. But the tip remained. An evil hour it was when he ever undertook to treat it! Then he took the white of an egg and bound it on the wound without doing anything further. He was unable to stop the wound from bleeding. He took juice of plantain and wild celery and fennel and salt and made a poultice of it and put it on the wound and stopped the flow. But the leg became blacker than coal. The suffering Tristan cried out and yelled night and day and carried on so until he felt of the wound and felt the spear point. And he called Isolt, his wife, and said to her,

"Lady, feel here, and you will feel the point which is making me suffer such pain, that the physician has not removed. For God's sake, send him to me straightway."

Then Isolt felt him and felt the point, and then the physician was sent for and he came immediately and pulled out the point. But much anguish and pain did the weary Tristan suffer from it.

When the point was out, the physician put an ointment on the wound, but it was for nought, for he knew nothing of his trade. And this was a great pity, for what he did to Tristan did nothing but harm him. The physicians who had come from all around labored hard to do for him what they thought would be good for him. Among them was a poor physician who had just recently come from the school at Salerno. When he saw these great masters, he said,

"Lords, you do not know what you are doing, for he will never be cured thus. The leg is all inflamed, and if the inflammation passes the joint, no one will ever be able to remedy it."

When the physicians heard this and saw him so poor, they began to show contempt, and they said,

"Ah, sire, how well you have your wits about you! They well become you!"

"Lords," he said, "I am poor, God shall give me enough when it pleases him. Nevertheless our wits are not in cloth or garb, but in our hearts where God has put them. But I shall go away, and you shall remain with this poor unfortunate, who will suffer the torments that you inflict on him, and you shall have the great gain of putting him to death, for I know certainly that he will not live long thus."

Then the physicians said that if he were not chased away they would all leave, for they would never remain there. Then the poor physician was pushed out, for you know that no one cares about a poor man anywhere.

And Isolt, Tristan's wife, gave him a mark of silver and dressed him well and equipped him and gave him a fine palfrey. Then he took leave and went away. Alas, what sorrow when he did not stay! For he would soon have healed him. The other physicians remained with Tristan, and labored hard to cure him. But it was in vain and for nought. And when they saw that they were wasting their efforts, they all departed in haste. And when Tristan saw this, he said very quietly through clenched teeth,

"God, what can I do when no physician can cure me? I know well, if I had someone to send word to the fair Isolt that she should come and heal me, that she would soon come, for she healed me once before."

Then he thought that there was in the town a sailor companion of his, named Genes. And he sent word that he should come and speak to him without delay, and Genes came and sat down before him.

"Genes," said Tristan, "fair, sweet fellow, I have summoned you here, for you can give me my health, if you will. I love you much, and know that, if I can come out of this, I shall give a very rich wedding to Isolt, your daughter and my goddaughter, and I shall give you much goods."

"Sire," said Genes, "command me and I shall do your command, on sea or on land."

"Genes," said Tristan, "a thousand thanks. You shall go to Cornwall, to Queen Isolt, my love, and you will tell her that I have sent for her to come and heal me, and you will tell her how I was wounded, and you will give her this ring, as proof that she should best believe you. And if she comes with you, see to it that the sail on your ship be white. And if you do not bring her, that it be black."

"Sire," said Genes, "most willingly shall I do this. My ship is now all ready and equipped in the port to go. But sire, I pray you concerning my daughter, your goddaughter."

"Certainly," said Tristan, "I shall watch over her as my own, and of this have not doubt. But think of my need."

Then Genes departed from Tristan and took his leave and went off to the port, where his ship was all loaded and ready, and he went aboard. And he ordered his men to weigh anchor and take the ship straight to Bomme in Cornwall. The sailors departed from the port and sailed day and night until they arrived at the port of Bomme. King Mark learned that a ship had arrived in port from Brittany, and he went to see what merchandise it had brought. When Genes saw King Mark, he left his ship and greeted him. The king asked him where he was from.

"Sire," said Genes, "I am a merchant from Brittany, and I bring goods to sell in your land, all of them at your command."

The king looked at Genes, who seemed most courteous to him, and he said to him,

"Brother, I wish and command that all the days of your stay here you come to my court at mealtimes. And I shall reserve all of your wines and have payment made to you now."

"Sire," said Genes, "a thousand thanks, but I shall not eat and drink outside my ship, save Your Grace. For I promised and swore to my wife when I left her that I would not take my ease in any other place."

Then the king laughed and said that he was a loyal man.

Then the king returned to the queen, and she asked where he had come from, and he told her that he had come from the port, where a ship had arrived from Brittany.

"I have reserved all his wines, but of all the other goods on the ship I desired nothing so ardently as a ring that the merchant to whom the ship belongs had on his finger."

"Sire," she asked, "what sort of ring is it?"

"Lady," he said. "I have never in my life seen one so fair. It is quite flat and there is an emerald in it, the fairest I have ever seen."

When the queen heard what the ring was like, she thought that it was the one she had given to Tristan and that it was some message that he had sent, and she said to the king,

"Sire, send word to the merchant that he should come and eat at your court."

"Lady," he said, "he would not come, to keep the pact that he made with his wife when he left. But I shall send word to him to come and speak to you, and you shall find out whether he would sell the ring."

"Sire," said the queen, "you have spoken well."

And then the king sent word to Genes that he should come and speak to the queen, and he came. When he had come before the king, he told him to go into the queen's chamber to speak to her, and Genes went in. All that was needed was to show him the way and take him there. When the queen saw Genes, she had him sit by her and she asked him where he was from.

"Lady," he said, "I am a native of Brittany, and I am a messenger from Tristan, who sends you greetings through me and who sends word to you to let nothing stop you from coming to heal him of a wound that Bedalis inflicted on him with a poisoned spear tip, from which he is dying in pain. And he will die if he has no help from you, for no physician can do anything. Instead, they have all left and abandoned him. In proof of this, here is the ring that you gave him when he gave you back to King Mark and you told him that you would believe nothing told to you of him if you did not see this ring."

"Faith," said the queen, "that is the truth, Genes. King Mark is leaving tomorrow morning for Cardwell, in Wales, to see King Arthur, who has sent for him. And when he has gone, I shall tell Andret that I wish to go hunting for small game, and I shall go off to this shore, and I shall ask him who owns your ship, as though I knew nothing of you. And he will tell me that it is your ship. And you be all ready to go and you shall tell me to come aboard your ship to see the goods on it. And a plank will be put down to the ship, on which I shall walk. But I pray you not to harm Andret."

"Lady," said Genes, "willingly."

Then he took leave and went away, and he left her the ring. Then the queen came to King Mark, her lord, and said that the merchant had given her his ring. The king thanked Genes much for it and did not fail to show him great gratitude for it, but it would have come out better for him had he dismissed him from his kingdom.

The next day early in the morning King Mark left to go and see King Arthur, who had sent for him. And when he had gone, Queen Isolt told Andret that she wished to go after small game, and he had the dogs and birds made ready. Then they mounted and went out into the fields. Many folk followed the queen. When they were in the fields, they flushed a pheasant. Andret released a falcon to catch it, but the falcon failed. The weather was clear and fair and the falcon took wing. The queen called Andret and said to him that the falcon had perched on the mast of the ship that she saw in the port, and she asked him to whom it belonged.

"Lady," said Andret, "that is the ship of Genes, the merchant from Brittany who gave you his ring yesterday."

"Let us go there," said the queen, "for our falcon."

And then they went off to the ship. Genes was off the ship and had put down a plank, and he came up to the queen and said,

"Lady, if it pleased you, you would come and see my ship and the goods aboard it. And if there is anything that pleases you, you may take it."

"Genes," said the queen, "a thousand thanks."

Then the queen dismounted and went by means of the plank straight to the ship and boarded it. Andret was going to her, but Genes, who was on the plank and holding an oar, struck Andret with the oar so that he knocked him into the water. Andret tried to hang on in order to pull himself out, and Genes struck him again with the oar and knocked him back into the sea and said,

"Cowardly traitor! Now you have your reward for the ill that you have made Tristan and Queen Isolt suffer so many times!"

Then he went aboard his ship and set sail from the port. Then was raised the hue and cry, and it was spread all around that Genes was carrying off the queen. And they all ran to the ships and the galleys and went after him. But it was for nought, for they were never able to reach them. And they turned back and found Andret, who was drowned, so much sea water had he drunk. And they pulled him out and buried him, for they could do nothing else. But now the tale ceases speaking of this and goes back to speak of Tristan.

THE DECEPTION OF THE SAILS

In this part the tale tells that after Genes had left Tristan to go and seek Queen Isolt, every day from morning till night Tristan was at the port of Penmarc to look at the ships coming and going, to learn whether he might see Genes's ship bringing Queen Isolt, his love, whom he desired so to see. He stayed there until he could no longer endure and went back away from all to lie in his chamber. His condition had become so bad that he could no longer stand on his feet nor eat nor drink. He felt more pain than ever before. His fainting spells came thick and fast. All around him wept in pity and great sorrow.

Tristan called his goddaughter, Genes's daughter, and said to her,

"Fair goddaughter, I love you much, and know that if I can recover from this illness I shall give you a fine, rich marriage. I pray you and wish that you keep silent about my secret and what I shall tell you. You shall go every morning to the bridge of Penmarc and stay there from morning until evening and look to see if your father's ship is coming. And I shall tell you how you will recognize it. If he is bringing Isolt, my love, whom I have sent

83

him to seek, the sail on his ship will be all white. And if he is not bringing her, it will be all black. Now take note of it if you see it and then come and tell me."

"Sire," said the maiden, "willingly."

The maiden went off to the port of Penmarc and was there all day, and she came to tell Tristan about all the ships that passed through there.

Isolt, Tristan's wife, wondered greatly about the maiden and why it was that she often sat thus all day long at the port and what it could be that she spoke so often about with Tristan. And she said that she would find out if she could. Then she went off to the port where her goddaughter was sitting and said to her,

"Goddaughter, I have lavished tender care on you in my chamber. I conjure you for God's sake to tell me why you are here like this every day."

"Lady," she said, "I cannot see, suffer, or hear the great torment and the great pain that my lord and godfather is suffering, and so I find solace here watching the ships come and go."

"Certainly," she said, "now I know that you have lied to me. And what are you so often talking about with your godfather? May God help me if you do not tell me, never more shall you remain with me. And if you do tell me, you shall be doing good."

The girl became frightened of her lady and said to her,

"Lady, my godfather has sent my father to Cornwall to seek Isolt, his love, in order to bring her here to heal him. If she comes, the sail on the ship will be all white, and if she does not come, it will be all black. And I am here to see whether I can see the ship coming, and if I saw it, I would go and tell my godfather."

When she heard these words, she became very angry and said,

"Alas, who would have thought that he might love another than I? Certainly they have never had as great joy of each other as I shall make them have sorrow and sadness!"

Then she looked down, far out to sea, and saw the ship coming with a white sail. Then she said to Tristan's goddaughter,

"I am going, and you shall remain here."

In great pain was Tristan. He could no longer eat nor drink, he neither heard nor understood anything. But nevertheless he called the abbot of Candon, who was in his presence with many others, and said to them,

"Fair lords, I shall hardly live much longer, I feel it clearly. I pray you, if ever you loved me, that when I am dead you put me on a ship and my sword beside me and this case. And then send me to Cornwall to King Mark, my uncle. And see to it that none read the letter which is hanging from my sword before I die."

Then he fainted. Then arose the lament in that place. And now his wicked wife came, bringing the evil news, and said,

"Ah, God! I have come from the port, and I have seen a ship coming here at full speed, and I think that we shall have it tonight here in this house."

When Tristan heard his wife speak of the ship, he opened his eyes and turned with great effort and said,

"For God's sake, sweet sister, tell me what the sail was like on the ship."

"Faith," she said, "it is blacker than a mulberry."

Alas, why did she say this? The Bretons must hate her so! As soon as he heard this, he knew that Isolt, his love, was not coming, and he turned away and said,

"Ah, sweet love, I commend you to God, never shall you see me, nor I you. May God watch over you. Be with God. I am going, and I bid you farewell."

Then he confessed himself and commended himself to God. And his heart burst in him and his soul departed.

Then began the lamenting and the sorrow in that place. The news spread through the town and the shore that Tristan had passed away. Then did great and small come running, screaming and shouting and lamenting so that one would not have heard God's thunder. Queen Isolt, who was at sea, said to Genes,

"I see folk running and I hear them screaming most sorely. I strongly suspect that the dream I dreamed last night may be true, for I dreamed that I was holding in my lap the head of a great boar that was staining me all over with its blood and making my robe all bloody. For God's sake, I fear greatly that Tristan may be dead. Make this boat ready and let us sail on straight to the port."

Genes placed her in the boat and they sailed straight on to dry land. When they had landed, she asked a squire who was weeping sorely what was the matter with him and where these folk were running with such purpose.

"Certainly, lady," he said, "I am weeping for Tristan, our lord, who died just now, and that is where all these folk you see are running."

When Isolt heard this, she fell to the ground in a faint, and Genes lifted her up. And when she had come to from her faint, they went on until they came to Tristan's chamber. And they found him dead, and the body was stretched out on a board. And the Countess of Montrelles was washing it and making it ready, and she had already put the slippers on it. When Isolt saw the body of Tristan, her love, there before her, she had the chamber emptied and let herself fall in a faint on the body. And when she came to from her faint, she felt his pulse and his vein, but it was for nought, for the soul had already departed some time before. Then she said,

"Sweet love, Tristan, what a sore separation is this of you and me! I had come to heal you. Now I have lost my way and my pains and you. And certainly, since you are dead, I no longer wish to live on after you. For since love has been between you and me for life, so must it be for death."

Then she held him in her arms against her bosom as tightly as she could, and she heaved a sigh, and her heart broke, and her soul departed. And so died the two lovers, Tristan and Isolt.

THE UNION OF TRISTAN AND ISOLT

When Genes saw this outcome, he rushed from the chamber, lamenting sorely, and said that Queen Isolt had died on Tristan's body. Then all ran to them and such great sorrow and lamenting began again that hardhearted would have been any who felt no pity for them. There was nothing else. The two bodies were put in their shrouds and made ready and counsel was taken as to how and where they would be buried.

"In the name of God," said the abbot of Candon, "Tristan told us that he had hung a letter on his sword and that when he was dead it should be read."

Then the sword was brought and the letter read, which said, as follows,

"Tristan commands all those who loved him to have his body taken to Cornwall to King Mark, his uncle, with his sword by his side, and that none be so bold as to open the case suspended from it until the king unlocks it and sees what is inside."

Then they agreed that the two bodies should be sent richly and honorably to Cornwall.

"But at least we shall keep the entrails."

Then Tristan was opened up and his entrails were taken and buried before the port, and a rich cross was fashioned there, and it was called Tristan's Cross. And they established a knight to guard it and keep it in repair every year, and he received a goodly income for this. And if he did not do so, he would lose his income. Then they embalmed the body and sewed it into a stag hide and Isolt into another. Then they placed the two bodies in a barrel on a ship, with two candles burning at their feet and two at their heads. And they placed crosses and phylacteries with them very richly, and the sword and case by Tristan's side, and then they commended the bodies to God.

The sailors boarded the ship and set sail and sailed until they arrived at the port below Tintagel. And they left the ship and removed the bodies from it and arranged them most honorably and placed the crosses and phylacteries at their heads and two at their feet. Then they covered them with two sheets of gold, most rich and most fair. There they found a little old woman, who had come from the mountains in the woods. When she saw the crosses and the bodies so richly laid out, she asked whose bodies they were. And the sailors answered that they were Tristan, King

Mark's nephew, and Isolt, the queen, King Mark's wife. When the
old woman heard this, she began the greatest lament that was ever
heard of woman. The sailors gave her ten sous to watch over the
bodies. Then they boarded their ship and returned to their country. But now the tale ceases speaking of this matter and speaks of
King Mark and his folk.

Now the tale tells that when the sailors had left the bodies in the
charge of the old woman, she began to weep and mourn for the
tales of Tristan and his deeds. The folk of the country came
running at the lamenting and crying and asked the old woman
whose bodies these were, and she told them that they were Tristan
and Isolt the fair, who was King Mark's wife. Then began such
great crying and lamenting that one would not have heard God's
thunder. There was a learned man there who read the letter which
said that none should be so bold as to unlock the case that hung
from the sword and that they should not be buried before King
Mark opened [it]. The folk of the country had walls put up around
the bodies and a chapel built. There they watched over the bodies
night and day, and they looked in common agreement to whom
they would send to seek King Mark, who had gone to Cardwell to
see King Arthur, who had sent for him. And they sent a hermit,
noble and who had lived a saintly life.

The hermit departed and traveled until he met King Mark at
Cachenes. He was bringing to Queen Isolt a little monkey which
King Arthur had sent her. Alas, he did not know that she was
dead, and Tristan, his nephew, also. The hermit greeted the king
and said,

"King, whoever takes his grief to heart and dies in anger leaves
God and gives body and soul to the Devil. And therefore I tell you
not to become angry on account of anything that you hear or see."

The king listened to the hermit preaching to him and said,

"If it pleases God, I shall never be so surprised that the Evil One
should have power over me. Say as much as you like in all assur-
ance of this."

"Sire," said the hermit, "you have answered most wisely.

Therefore I shall tell you. Know for certain that Tristan, your nephew, and Isolt, your wife, are dead. And they have been sent to you from Brittany. And there are a letter and a case suspended from Tristan's sword, forbidding anyone to be so bold as to unlock the case except you. And know that Tristan was ill of a wound which none could heal but Isolt. And he sent for her through Genes, who took her away. But before she arrived there, Tristan died, and she too died of grief. And their bodies have been sent to you for the sake of God. They have been at the port now nearly three days. Therefore hasten and see what is in the case, and then do with the bodies according to your will."

When the king heard this news, he was overcome with grief and would have fallen off his horse if the hermit had not held him up, and he said,

"Ah, Tristan, fair nephew, so much pain have you made me suffer! You have put me to shame and have taken my wife. Never by my father's soul shall you be buried in my country."

Then the king rode on until he came to the port of Tintagel where the bodies were. The people learned of the oath that the king had sworn, and they all shouted with one voice,

"Ah, king, take all we have, but inter honorably him who took you and your country and us from the servitude we were in and freed us, as you know full well."

When the king heard the people cry out, he had pity on them. And he took the case and unlocked it. And in it was a letter written and sealed with Tristan's seal. The king had the archbishop read the letter, which said,

"To his dear uncle, King Mark of Cornwall, Tristan, his nephew, greetings. Sire, you sent me to Ireland to seek Isolt, your wife. When I had won her and she was delivered to me to bring to you, her mother had a keg of herbed wine prepared which was of such a nature that he who drank of it had to love her who drank of it after him, and she him. Sire, know that this keg was given to Brangien to keep, and she was forbidden to let anyone drink of it but you and Isolt, the night after you had married her and you were to sleep together. Sire, when we had put to sea, it was so hot that it seemed as though the whole world would stifle. And a very great thirst seized me, and I asked for something to drink. And Brangien, who was not paying attention, gave me something to drink, and I drank, and Isolt after me, so that never afterward was there an hour when we did not love each other. Sire, for God's sake, see that there was a reason that I could not help myself if I loved Isolt, when I did so by force. Now do with this as it pleases you."

"Sire," said the archbishop, "concerning what is in this letter, what is your will?"

When King Mark heard that Tristan had loved Isolt through the force of the herbed wine and that it had not been out of his free will, he was overcome with sorrow and anger, and he began to weep and said,

"Alas, wretch that I am, why did I not know of this adventure? I would rather have concealed and approved of them than have him now gone from me! Alas, now I have lost my nephew and my wife!"

Then he commanded that the bodies be brought to the chapel and interred there as richly as is appropriate for highborn folk. The king had two coffins made, one of chalcedony and the other of beryl. Tristan was placed in the one made of chalcedony and Isolt in the one of beryl, and they were buried amid weeping and tears, one on one side of the chapel and the other on the other side.

Perinis, who was lying ill, heard the noise, and he rose and came to where the crying was. When he learned that Tristan and Isolt, his lady, were dead and buried there, he began to lament so over the tombs that none who saw him did not take pity on him. And he said that he would never leave there except in death. The king had a little dwelling made for him there when he saw that he would not leave the spot. Hudein, Tristan's dog, had gone into the forest and had found many hinds, but he never let himself be turned aside by them, and he ran straight to the port where the bodies had been at first, and he began to bark and howl. And he came by means of their traces straight to the chapel where the bodies had been buried. As soon as he saw Perinis, he ran to him, and he smelled from the traces that his master's body was buried there, and he began to run around and howl so violently that all marveled at it. There stayed Hudein and Perinis, without eat or drink, and when they had done their lamenting over Tristan, they went and mourned over Isolt.

Perinis sent word by a messenger to Gouvernal and Brangien in Lyonesse. As soon as they learned the news, they mounted and rode until they came to Cornwall and found Perinis and Hudein in the chapel where the bodies were buried. As soon as Gouvernal saw Hudein, he knew full well that the body of his lord was buried there and that where Perinis was Isolt was buried.

From inside Tristan's tomb there emerged a bramble, fair and green and leafy, which rose over the chapel. And the tip of the bramble descended to Isolt's tomb and entered it. The folk of the country saw this and told the king. The king had it cut down three times. The next day it was there again, as fair and in the same state as it had been before. This miracle took place over Tristan and over Isolt. Gouvernal and Brangien began to weep and mourn for Tristan, their lord, and Isolt, their lady. King Mark tried to retain Gouvernal and Brangien with him and make them lords and masters of his land. But they would not stay. Instead they took leave and took back with them Perinis and Hudein. Gouvernal was king of Lyonesse and Brangien queen, and they made Perinis seneschal of all their land and lived together until God desired to take them to him. So may he do with us! *Amen!*

Here ends the Romance of Tristan and Isolt.